What It Takes to Operate and Maintain Principal Pipelines

Costs and Other Resources

Julia H. Kaufman | Susan M. Gates | Melody Harvey | Yan Wang | Mark Barrett

Commissioned by

The Wallace Foundation

Supporting ideas.
Sharing solutions.
Expanding opportunities.

RAND CORPORATION

For more information on this publication, visit www.rand.org/t/RR2078

Library of Congress Cataloging-in-Publication Data is available for this publication

ISBN: 978-0-8330-9845-0

Published by the RAND Corporation, Santa Monica, Calif.

Front cover image: Kurhan/Fotolia
Back cover image: Gelpi/Fotolia

Preface

The Wallace Foundation is committed to improving school leadership. To further this objective, it began the Principal Pipeline Initiative. The initiative supports efforts in six districts across the United States to develop principal pipelines through engagement in activities related to the preparation, hiring, development, evaluation, and support of school leaders. Policy Studies Associates and the RAND Corporation are conducting the evaluation of the initiative. Five reports by Policy Studies Associates document the Principal Pipeline Initiative's theory of action and its implementation (The Wallace Foundation, undated). An evaluation of the initiative's effects on student achievement and other outcomes will be released in December 2018.

This report supplements the Principal Pipeline Initiative implementation reports by describing the resources and expenditures devoted to principal pipelines in the districts participating in the initiative. The report first presents a framework for thinking about the full range of resources and expenditures associated with principal pipelines. Then it provides estimates of these pipeline resources and expenditures based on the experience of participating districts, setting them in a broader context of district expenditures for supporting school district personnel. Although it is too early to tell whether the investments that participating districts made are improving school outcomes, this report lays the groundwork for future considerations of return on investment when more information on the initiative's effects is available.

This report will be of special interest to school districts and state education agencies around the country given expanded opportunities through the Every Student Succeeds Act (Pub. L. 114-95, 2015) to use federal funds to support initiatives to improve school leadership (Herman et al., 2017). The information in this report could help school districts and state education agencies consider potential investments in principal pipelines that could be procured through federal funding.

This research has been conducted by RAND Education, a division of the RAND Corporation, with grant funding from The Wallace Foundation. For more about RAND Education, visit www.rand.org/education.

Contents

Exhibits

Boxes

Figures

Tables

Summary

States and districts are embarking on efforts to improve school leadership as a lever to promote school improvement. Such efforts have a solid base of research attesting to their effectiveness (Herman et al., 2017), and some view them as particularly cost-effective because principals "can be powerful multipliers of effective teaching and leadership practices in schools" (Manna, 2015, p. 7; Leithwood et al., 2004, p. 14). Although the logic of this perspective is sound, in truth, we know very little about the resources required to improve school leadership.

This report fills an important gap in the literature on school leadership by (1) presenting an approach for understanding the resources and expenditures associated with efforts to prepare, hire, evaluate, develop, and support school leaders and by (2) presenting estimates of those resources and expenditures. All districts that employ more than a few school leaders devote at least some resources to these activities and might find some value to our approach. We apply our approach to develop estimates of the resources required to put in place and operate *principal pipelines*—pipelines for preparing, hiring, supporting, and managing school leaders—based on data we collected from six urban districts that participated in The Wallace Foundation's Principal Pipeline Initiative.

Investments in Principal Pipelines

School leaders are the people engaged in the day-to-day work of overseeing schools. Principal pipelines are composed of the activities that districts undertake to ensure that school leadership is effective and is meeting the district's needs. In that sense, the entirety of district spending on the preparation, hiring, evaluation, development, and support of school leaders can be viewed as an investment. The Principal Pipeline Initiative catalyzed districts to make investments to develop principal pipelines with clearly defined characteristics. In this report, we use the term *investment* to describe the resources that participating districts devoted to the enhancements necessary to create coherent principal pipelines, as the initiative defines them, while recognizing that all resources devoted to principal pipelines could also be considered an investment in schools and students. Box S.1 provides a brief overview of the initiative and a definition of the principal pipeline.

Box S.1

The Principal Pipeline Initiative

Informed by more than a decade of work on school leadership and the surrounding structures that support it, The Wallace Foundation posited that public districts in the United States could improve school leadership through systematic improvements to a core set of activities related to the preparation, hiring, support, and management of school leaders. The foundation launched the Principal Pipeline Initiative in 2011 to test that hypothesis. The initiative defined four key components of a principal pipeline: (1) leadership standards that guide all pipeline activities; (2) preservice preparation opportunities for assistant principals (APs) and principals (including not only the preservice training itself but also recruitment and selection into these opportunities); (3) selective hiring and placement; and (4) on-the-job induction, evaluation, and support. In addition, the initiative aimed to develop capacity, culture, and infrastructure to sustain the work across components. The foundation initially awarded $7.5 million to $12.5 million to six large urban school districts to cover part of the costs of setting up principal pipelines. In 2014, it provided additional funding of $430,000 to $1 million per district to support improvements in principal supervision. Each of the six districts selected for the initiative had emphasized school leadership as part of its school reform agenda and had already devoted some attention to the preparation, hiring, evaluation, or support of principals prior to the launch of the initiative. Each district also had a desire to "further strengthen and align these functions" (Turnbull, Riley, Arcaira, et al., 2013, p. 3). Participating districts varied in terms of both the aspects of their principal pipelines on which they intended to focus most and their starting points.

A series of reports documents findings from the evaluation of implementation of the Principal Pipeline Initiative (The Wallace Foundation, 2015–2017). A study of the initiative's effects on student and other outcomes is scheduled for release at the end of 2018.

Investments in principal pipelines could demonstrate value for school districts by improving the quality of school leaders and reducing unwanted principal turnover. These investments not only could affect the principalship itself but could also conceivably have a positive impact on all teachers and students in a school, leading to improvements in

- school climate
- stakeholder satisfaction
- student outcomes
- unwanted teacher turnover and the costs associated with it
- future district costs associated with the preparation and management of school leaders.

These investments could also lower future district costs associated with the preparation and management of school leaders.

It is too early to assess whether these payoffs have been realized, but early evidence from studies of implementation of the initiative (Turnbull, Anderson, et al., 2016) is encouraging. In addition, preliminary analysis of available data from districts participating in the initiative suggests that, in three of the participating districts, the percentage of newly hired principals who continue to serve as principals in the district after two years increased substantially between school year (SY) 2010–2011 and SY 2013–2014. As ongoing research generates more evidence regarding the effects of investments in the initiative, the estimates of the resources required to develop and operate principal pipelines can serve as guidance for district decisionmaking about whether certain investments in the principal pipeline are worthwhile.

Approach

Our objectives for this study were twofold: (1) to develop a framework for estimating the resources and expenditures of developing and operating principal pipelines and (2) to provide clear information to school districts and other stakeholders regarding estimates of those costs. We gathered data on the resources and expenditures associated with principal pipeline activities in the six school districts that received funding from The Wallace Foundation through the Principal Pipeline Initiative. Our data-gathering and analyses took into account both costs of personnel and costs of other expenditures and resources that school districts assumed to develop and manage pipelines, including costs for materials, hardware, software, consultants, and other expenditures associated with principal pipeline activities. The cost estimates presented in our report are intended to inform school districts around the country about what it could take to build and operate a strong principal pipeline. Recognizing that other districts might not have the capacity to undertake investment in the entire pipeline at one time, we strived to provide estimates of overall principal pipeline costs in the participating districts *and* estimates for the costs of individual categories and activities associated with principal pipelines.

In our data-gathering and analysis, we used an activity-based approach (Kaplan and Cooper, 1998; Miles et al., 2004; Chambers, Lam, and Mahitivanichcha, 2008). Guided by this activity-based approach, we developed a list of activities that could be associated with principal pipelines. We categorized each activity under one of the four components of a principal pipeline, as described above. We also gathered information on systems of support for a comprehensive principal pipeline, which made up a fifth category of activities. We divided some activities within major categories into subactivities. The resulting list of activities and subactivities is provided in Table S.1.

This list of activities guided our data-collection process and can serve as a practical resource to other districts by helping them identify what pieces of their principal

Table S.1
Principal Pipeline Activities and Subactivities, by Major Category

Category	Component	Activity	Subactivity
Pipeline component	1. Leader standards	Develop or revise leader standards and secure their approval.	—
	2. Preservice preparation	Revise the system of preservice preparation.	Develop internal, district-led preservice courses.[a] Develop external program or university-based courses.[a] Develop screening and selection processes.[a] Prepare and train personnel to use the new screening and selection processes.
		Recruit principal and AP candidates for preservice preparation.	—
		Screen and select candidates for preservice preparation.[a]	—
		Deliver preservice preparation.	Deliver internal, district-led preparation.[a] Deliver external contractor- or partner-led preparation.[a]
		Oversee the quality of the portfolio of preservice preparation programs.	Conduct a Quality Measures review.[b] Oversee the quality of preservice preparation (beyond Quality Measures).
	3. Selective hiring and placement	Revise the system for principal recruiting, hiring, and placement (design processes and train personnel).	—
		Recruit principal and AP candidates.	—
		Screen, select, and support the candidate pool.[a]	—
		Interview and hire school leaders.[a]	—

Table S.1—Continued

Category	Component	Activity	Subactivity
	4. On-the-job support and evaluation	Revise the system for providing on-the-job support and evaluation for principals and APs.	Design new on-the-job support and induction processes and courses and provide personnel training. Design new evaluation processes, including technology, and provide personnel training.
		Provide on-the-job support and induction for principals and APs.	Provide induction and first-year on-the-job PD.[a] Provide on-the-job PD after the first year.[a] Provide schoolwide support via teams and networks. Support the implementation of SAM.[c]
		Evaluate principals and APs.	Evaluate principals and APs aside from the use of the Vanderbilt Assessment of Leadership in Education.[d] Evaluate principals using the Vanderbilt Assessment of Leadership in Education.
		Provide executive coaching and support to those who supervise and support principals.	—
Systems and capacity for supporting the pipeline components		Revise the overall principal pipeline.	—
		Develop and disseminate communication about the initiative.	—
		Develop and maintain an LTS.	—
		Oversee implementation of the pipeline (quality assurance).	—

NOTE: LTS = leader tracking system. PD = professional development. SAM = School Administration Manager.

[a] Separate activity or subactivity for principals and for APs.

[b] Quality Measures is a tool that the Education Development Center developed, with support from The Wallace Foundation, to improve partnerships between school districts and principal preservice providers.

[c] SAM is a daily PD set of practices designed to help leaders increase time spent on instructional-leadership activities and reflect on impact and next steps. The National SAM Innovation Project developed it with support from The Wallace Foundation.

[d] The Vanderbilt Assessment of Leadership in Education is a principal-evaluation tool for assessing principal behaviors. Vanderbilt University developed it with support from The Wallace Foundation.

pipelines are already in place within their districts and what additional activities they might consider undertaking. It is important to note that this list does not represent all the activities in which districts should engage in order to have a robust principal pipeline. Participating districts engaged in the activities on this list at different levels (and sometimes not at all), depending on their goals and vision. Likewise, districts using this activity list as a resource should consider which activities are feasible for them and align with their vision for enhancing their principal pipeline. Funding from The Wallace Foundation supported district efforts to enhance principal pipeline activities, but districts devoted substantial resources of their own to their pipelines throughout the initiative. Our analysis of costs for principal pipeline activities accounts for but is not limited to resources that The Wallace Foundation provided.

Data Sources

Principal pipeline costs are not a line item in school budget and expenditure reports. For our study, we gathered information about the costs of activities through multiple data sources. The data sources for our study included the following:

- **District principal pipeline expenditure reports.** Each participating district provided these to The Wallace Foundation on principal pipeline–related spending over the course of the initiative—from August 2011 through December 2015.
- **Expenditure reports for technical assistance.** The Wallace Foundation also collected expenditure reports from consultants and organizations with which they contracted to provide guidance to districts for aspects of the Principal Pipeline Initiative, which we used to identify technical assistance work that was key to districts' pipeline work.
- **In-depth interviews with district personnel.** We collected these to resolve questions about information provided in district expenditure reports and identify gaps in the information about expenditures provided in those reports.
- **District personnel resource-allocation data.** We collected these to account for the value of the time that district personnel spent on principal pipeline activities.
- **Survey data.** Policy Studies Associates administered surveys in 2014 and 2015 as part of its implementation evaluation efforts (Turnbull, Anderson, et al., 2016).
- **District proposals, budgets, and progress reports.** Each participating district provided these to The Wallace Foundation.

Scope

We provide estimates of how much the participating districts spend on pipeline activities in a baseline preinitiative year and in five years that span the initiative. Our estimates of preinitiative spending on these same activities, although rough, provide information on business as usual in these districts. Our study focused on the resources and expenditures associated with district efforts to support school leadership, not the totality of resources devoted to school leadership itself. We focused on the resources expended by districts, not other stakeholders. As a result, we excluded from consideration the salary costs of the school leaders themselves. We recognize that school leaders might participate in the preparation or management of other school leaders, which might be expected to vary because of differences in conditions related to the market for school leaders. In cases in which a school leader was paid a stipend beyond salary in order to take on additional responsibilities to support the principal pipeline, we include those costs.

Table S.2 provides an overview of all the decisions we made about what to include in and exclude from our cost estimates. In Chapter Two of this report, we provide more detail on the associated challenges and limitations that each decision presented.

After using our activity list to categorize resources and expenditures—and making final decisions about what costs to include—we generated district-by-district summaries of pipeline costs. We transformed these summary data to account for regional variation in purchasing power (i.e., cost of living) and inflation during the time period. After adjusting for cost of living, we also adjusted costs in each district depending on various drivers, and we present costs by various cost drivers throughout this report, focusing particularly on costs per principal.

Table S.2
Costs Included in and Excluded from Our Estimates

Included	Excluded
• Costs that schools districts themselves bore, including cost of personnel time and other direct costs (e.g., materials, software) • Costs of work funded through both The Wallace Foundation and other funding sources • Costs of time for district personnel who supported principal pipeline efforts, including those across multiple offices (e.g., human resources, leadership, information technology) • Costs of schoolwide supports that also provided direct and explicit support to principals • Costs for technology that supported the pipeline (e.g., hardware and software necessary for LTSs)	• Costs that outside consultants or subcontracts bore beyond what the district paid for those services • Costs of time for principals and APs who took part in pipeline activities (excluding payments on top of salaries to those supporting the pipeline) • Opportunity costs of district personnel time, beyond estimates for the cost of personnel time for individual activities • Costs of schoolwide supports that did not explicitly support principals • New York City resources and expenditures for two major categories for which data were unavailable: (1) selective hiring and placement and (2) on-the-job support and evaluation

Findings

For all categories of principal pipeline activities and across all years of the Principal Pipeline Initiative, districts spent about $5.6 million each year, on average, which translated to a little more than $31,000 per principal or $42 per pupil per year. We calculated per-principal and per-pupil costs simply by dividing the total cost by the number of principals or pupils in each district and then calculating the average per-principal or per-pupil cost across districts. For all of these districts, pipeline costs represented just a small fraction of total expenditures in each year (0.4 percent). We estimate that a little less than half of the principal pipeline spending (or about $14,000 per principal) is devoted to on-the-job support and evaluation of principals and APs. To put these numbers into context, a 2015 study by The New Teacher Project indicated that districts spent between $10,000 and $26,000 per teacher per year and between 5 and 10 percent of all district expenditures on teacher PD. We are not aware of any studies that assess the full cost of teacher pipelines, including teacher PD.

Spending on principal pipeline activities changed considerably over time across participating districts. In the year prior to the initiative's launch, we estimate that districts were spending, on average, a little less than $9,400 per principal on these activities, although our estimate for the preinitiative period might exclude relevant costs that the districts did not track. In the first year of the initiative (SY 2011–2012), we estimate that average annual principal pipeline costs were $20,264 per principal. From SY 2011–2012 to SY 2014–2015, average costs steadily grew to nearly $37,000 per principal and then declined somewhat in SY 2015–2016.

Districts spent much more on the preservice and on-the-job support and evaluation categories of the principal pipeline (about $9,400 and $14,000 per principal, respectively) than on other categories, and the range of costs of those activities across districts—in particular, the range of preservice costs—was much larger than the ranges for the other pipeline categories. The higher cost and large range for preservice and on-the-job support costs reflected the very different strategies and preservice programs that the districts pursued. In contrast, the cost of the leader standards component was particularly small, at only $292 per principal or about $90,300 annually.

We summarize key findings by pipeline category in the rest of this section.

Leader Standards

The Principal Pipeline Initiative implementation studies that Policy Studies Associates conducted identified leader standards as a "quick win" (Turnbull, Anderson, et al., 2016, p. 29) for participating districts. Each district developed and used leader standards as a tool to guide many aspects of pipeline work. Our study shows that these activities came with a relatively small price tag:

- On average, districts devoted a small share of total pipeline resources to leader standards, amounting to $292 per principal or $0.41 per pupil.
- Leader standards work was not a one-time proposition; districts devoted resources to leader standards in each year of the initiative.
- Some districts front-loaded their leader standards work early in the initiative, whereas other emphasized this work toward the end of the initiative.
- More than 80 percent of the costs of leader standards efforts reflected costs for personnel time to develop and refine the standards.
- A district's starting point on leader standards seemed to influence total district spending on leader standards, while district size was not related to leader standards work.

Preservice Preparation

The Principal Pipeline Initiative implementation studies found that districts took varied approaches to strengthen their role in principal preparation and to align program features with research-based recommendations for high-quality preservice preparation (see Turnbull, Anderson, et al., 2016, p. 15). Turnbull, Anderson, et al., also noted that the time between the start of principal preservice and placement as a principal in a participating district ranged from three to ten years, suggesting that it will take time to fully assess the implications of enhanced preservice preparation (Turnbull, Anderson, et al., 2016). Our study revealed wide variation across districts in the resources devoted to these efforts:

- On average, districts devoted a substantial share of total pipeline resources to preservice preparation, amounting to $9,386 per principal or $13.27 per pupil.
- A little more than three-quarters of all costs for the preservice component were devoted to the delivery of preservice preparation.
- Districts adopted vastly different approaches to supporting preservice preparation, and this is reflected in wide variation in spending for preservice activities across districts.
- Stipends provided to those participating in principal residencies that were a part of some preservice programs represented a large portion of the costs for those programs.

Selective Hiring and Placement

All Principal Pipeline Initiative districts undertook efforts to make hiring and placement processes more systematic, rooted in leader standards and guided by objective data. According to the initiative implementation studies, top district leaders viewed the changes made to hiring and placement during the Principal Pipeline Initiative as successful (Turnbull, Anderson, et al., 2016, p. 25). Our study indicates that these efforts, like leader standards efforts, had relatively low costs associated with them:

- On average, districts devoted a small share of total pipeline resources to selective hiring and placement: $2,894 per principal or $3.57 per pupil.
- Nearly half of the resources devoted to hiring and placement during the initiative were investments in revisions to hiring systems.
- Compared with other pipeline categories, the range of costs for hiring and placement across districts was narrow; much of the variation stemmed from differences in resources devoted to system improvements.

On-the-Job Support and Evaluation

According to Turnbull, Anderson, et al., 2016, all participating districts took measures to improve principal supervision, and several districts expanded access to principal and AP coaching and mentoring, although districts differed in terms of the mix of school leader supports they provided, as well as the intensity and duration of those supports (Turnbull, Anderson, et al., 2016). Surveys suggest that new principals appreciated the one-on-one mentoring, coaching, and on-the-job support that principal supervisors provided (Turnbull, Anderson, et al., 2016, pp. 37–47):

- On average, districts devoted nearly half of their total pipeline resources to on-the-job support and evaluation (47 percent), amounting to $13,956 per principal or $18.53 per pupil.
- The vast majority of these resources were devoted to the provision of on-the-job support for principals and APs: Districts devoted nearly $11,000 per principal to these activities.
- Main costs for on-the-job support included coaching and mentoring, principal supervision, the SAM process, costs for consultants, and materials and supplies necessary for delivering ongoing PD for school leaders.

Systems of Support

The initiative implementation studies found that each of the participating districts also devoted staff and other resources to activities that cut across the four initiative components. Our study identified costs associated with four of those cross-cutting activities: efforts to revise the principal pipeline, oversee the implementation of pipeline activities, develop and maintain LTSs, and engage in communication about the pipeline:

- The development and maintenance of LTSs was the largest contributor to costs for systems of support, at almost $2,000 per principal each year, on average.

- Spending on LTSs over the course of the initiative was not related to any metric of district size.
- All districts invested at least some resources and expenditures in communications about the initiative, and most hired consultants or others to help them plan communication strategies and messaging about initiative efforts.

District Personnel Time

The cost for district personnel time made up nearly half, or about 44 percent, of spending devoted to all pipeline activities. District personnel time accounted for a particularly large portion of total costs for two pipeline categories: development of leader standards and hiring and placement activities.

As is true of all resources, time that district staff spent on pipeline activities has *opportunity costs* associated with it. Opportunity costs are defined as "benefit[s] that a person could have received, but gave up, to take another course of action" ("Opportunity Cost," undated). All staff members have limited time available. For example, when a principal is pulled out of school for a day to screen school leader candidates in a hiring pool, that principal is not in the school building supporting teachers and students. The value of what the principal would have been doing in the school that day is the opportunity cost of the principal's participation in the hiring pool screening.

The concept of opportunity cost also applies to the time of central district personnel. Costs associated with central district personnel time were highest for on-the-job evaluation and support activities. Principal supervisors, as well as other district personnel, contributed to these evaluation and support activities.

During the initiative, all districts increased the amount of supervisory time on pipeline activities by increasing the number of principal supervisors overall or increasing the share of their time devoted to pipeline-related activities. Although the share of time that principal supervisors contributed to different activities in the pipeline changed very little over the course of the initiative, total supervisory time on each activity increased. Districts that wish to invest further in their principal pipelines might need to be particularly strategic in how they reconfigure district personnel time and assign district staff to work on principal pipeline activities.

Conclusions

For districts that might be interested in developing a principal pipeline, our analysis provides a sense of the investment required to do the work at the district level to promote strong leadership in schools.

Our study shows that principal pipelines are not a big-ticket item for school districts. On average, over the course of the Principal Pipeline Initiative, participating districts devoted 0.4 percent of their current expenditures to principal pipeline activities, during a time when they were making active investments to build, as well as operate, pipelines.

Pipeline districts devoted the vast majority of pipeline resources to preservice and on-the-job support and evaluation activities. These two categories of the pipeline accounted for roughly three-quarters of all spending on principal pipelines, on average. Perhaps more interesting for districts considering their own pipeline efforts is the finding that participating districts devoted modest resources to the development and revision of leader standards and to selective hiring and placement efforts—$0.41 per pupil ($292 per principal) and $3.57 per pupil ($2,894 per principal), respectively. These are activities that Turnbull, Anderson, et al., described as quick wins, having high impact in participating districts (Turnbull, Anderson, et al., 2016). The findings thus suggest that a district does not need an infusion of substantial grant funding to make real progress on important aspects of principal pipelines. That said, leader standards development and selective hiring and placement were also areas in which the cost of district personnel time represented a large portion of all necessary resources and expenditures. So even though funding might not be a constraint in getting initiatives in these areas off the ground, district staff time could be.

Participating districts devoted at least some resources toward systems and capacity to support principal pipelines, including the development and maintenance of LTSs (data systems designed to support improved preparation, hiring, and support of school leaders). Districts reported LTSs to be very useful, but their development required investments that varied a fair amount by district and by year, depending on the data resources that had already been developed in the district.

Our analysis revealed substantial variation across districts—and within districts over time—in terms of spending on preservice and on-the-job support. Readers might wonder whether there are lessons in that variation that point to cost-effective practices for preservice preparation and on-the-job support. Unfortunately, our study cannot provide definitive answers to that question. However, we did observe that cost variation was influenced by the way in which a district configured its pipeline; the share of the full cost of certain activities that the district funded; the activities it chose to emphasize during the initiative; and the characteristics of the district context, such as the depth of a district's pool of principal candidates. The initiative specified broad categories of activities that the districts were expected to undertake but, within those broad categories, granted districts substantial flexibility regarding the specific activities. With regard to both preservice and on-the-job support and evaluation, participating districts engaged in a substantial amount of experimentation, as reflected by the share of costs devoted to these activities that were characterized as investment in pipeline enhancements rather than ongoing costs. Over the course of the initiative, spending increased for both preservice and on-the-job support and evaluation, although on-the-job support costs were more stable, whereas preservice costs declined toward the end of the initiative. The cause of the decline in preservice costs is unclear. It could be that some costs were short-term investments to increase the size of the pool or to pilot-test preservice preparation activities that did not work out as expected. Alternatively, districts might have identified more cost-efficient ways to provide preservice preparation activities.

By providing estimates of resources and expenditures for individual principal pipeline activities, this study provides important input for districts that are considering improvements to activities within their own principal pipelines. Coupled with information generated by a future study of the initiative's effects, these estimates will aid districts in making strategic choices about investments to improve and strengthen their principal pipelines.

Acknowledgments

This report draws on multiple sources of data about six school districts that participated in The Wallace Foundation's Principal Pipeline Initiative, and we are indebted to many people who contributed to the research in a variety of ways. First and foremost, we would like to thank staff members in the participating districts who provided us with input on our conceptual framework, responded to many rounds of data collection over the course of this project, and validated our coding of the data at multiple points throughout the study. This study would not have been possible without their input. We would also like to thank Aiesha Eleusizov of The Wallace Foundation, who provided us with expenditure information from foundation grantees and responded to numerous rounds of questions about the data. In addition, this research benefited from feedback from superintendents of the participating districts and other district staff beyond our points of contact.

We also leveraged a collaboration with Policy Studies Associates (PSA) to gather data through surveys to principals and assistant principals, as well as interviews with district staff that PSA was undertaking for the evaluation of implementation of the initiative. We appreciate the collaboration and support we received from Brenda J. Turnbull and Jaclyn MacFarlane of PSA to coordinate these efforts. Brenda also provided helpful feedback on a prior draft of this report. We would also like to thank the senior staff from participating districts who participated in interviews and the principals and assistant principals who participated in surveys.

Heather L. Schwartz of RAND provided guidance on the conceptual framework and data collection. Numerous RAND colleagues provided feedback on our conceptual framework. Paul Youngmin Yoo of RAND cleaned and analyzed some of the cost data for this study.

We would also like to thank our contacts at The Wallace Foundation who provided substantial input into the design of this study and the communication of findings. In particular, we have benefited from feedback from Elizabeth Ty Wilde, Will Miller, Jody Spiro, Aiesha Eleusizov, Nicholas Pelzer, Rochelle Herring, Edward Pauly, Lucas Bernays Held, Pamela Mendels, and Jessica Schwartz. Lynn A. Karoly of RAND and Henry M. Levin of Columbia University provided helpful feedback on an earlier version of this report. Donna White helped to compile and format the final document. Lisa Bernard and Blair Smith provided a careful edit of the final draft.

We take full responsibility for any errors.

Abbreviations

AP	assistant principal
CMO	charter management organization
CPI-U	Consumer Price Index for All Urban Consumers
DOE	Department of Education (specific to New York City)
HR	human resources
LTS	leader tracking system
MSA	metropolitan statistical area
NCES	National Center for Education Statistics
ODC	other direct cost
PD	professional development
PSA	Policy Studies Associates
RPP	regional price parity
SAM	School Administration Manager
SY	school year
VAL-ED	Vanderbilt Assessment of Leadership in Education

CHAPTER ONE

Introduction

Effective school leadership has tremendous potential to improve outcomes for students and promote excellence in schools. A high-quality leader in just one school could potentially improve the performance of dozens of teachers and hundreds or thousands of students. An effective leader in every school could be a means of supporting high-quality teaching in every classroom across a district or state. In contrast, ineffective leaders might be unable to help teachers improve their craft and could drive away talented teachers. Ultimately, students suffer when schools have poor leaders.

Districts can increase the chances of student success through a range of efforts to more effectively prepare and support school leaders. The Every Student Succeeds Act (Pub. L. 114-95), signed into law in 2015 as a reauthorization of the federal Elementary and Secondary Education Act (Pub. L. 89-10, 1965), emphasizes the importance of school leadership for school improvement and provides opportunities for states and districts to use federal funds to support initiatives intended to improve the quality of principals and other school leaders. In selecting or designing school leadership initiatives, states and districts can draw from a solid base of research that is consistent with the requirements of the Every Student Succeeds Act, demonstrating a link between such initiatives and positive outcomes for students, schools, teachers, or principals (Herman et al., 2017). This research base can be used to support initiatives involving leader-evaluation systems, principal preparation programs, strategic staff management, professional learning for principals and other school leaders, school leader working conditions, and broader school improvement efforts that have a leadership focus.

Despite their demonstrated potential, efforts to improve the quality of school leadership can be a tough sell for districts and states.[1] In an era of serious resource constraints, stakeholder pressures encourage states and districts to spend money directly on students or teachers and make it difficult to justify expenditures on support for principals (see, for example, Smith, 2011). Often overlooked are the costs that districts (not to mention teachers and students) bear when they have to replace principals in quick succession or make do with inadequate leaders. Furthermore, the ongoing costs

[1] We use the term *district* to describe both traditional school districts and charter management organizations (CMOs).

of poor school leadership are less visible but arguably more significant than the costs of replacing school leaders. Higher teacher turnover, worsening school climate conditions, and declines in student achievement are all outcomes that can be tied to poor leadership (Johnson and Birkland, 2003; Leithwood et al., 2004).

More than a decade ago, Leithwood et al. concluded that "efforts to improve [school leader] recruitment, training, evaluation and ongoing development should be considered highly cost-effective approaches to successful school improvement" (Leithwood et al., 2004, p. 14). But even now, we know very little about the resources required to effectively prepare, hire, evaluate, develop, and support school leaders. One study estimated that districts might typically spend about $75,000 to "develop, hire and onboard" a principal (School Leaders Network, 2014, p. 4), but the resulting report does not elaborate on the methods for developing such estimates. A small number of studies have examined the costs of teacher professional development (PD) in particular, although they do not examine the costs of the entire pipeline for preparing, hiring, supporting, and evaluating teachers.[2]

In this report, we describe an approach for understanding the resources and expenditures associated with district efforts to prepare and manage school leaders. Throughout, we use the term *manage* as shorthand for a range of talent management activities, including preservice preparation, hiring, evaluation, PD, and support once on the job (George W. Bush Institute, 2016). We also present estimates of the resources required to develop, manage, and operate principal pipelines (defined below) based on data we collected from six districts that participated in The Wallace Foundation's Principal Pipeline Initiative (described in Box 1.1). As we describe below, funding from The Wallace Foundation supported efforts in six large urban school districts to develop principal pipelines. These districts had been devoting resources to activities associated with principal pipelines prior to the launch of the initiative and continued to devote substantial resources of their own to principal pipelines throughout the initiative. As such, our analysis accounts for but is not limited to resources provided by The Wallace Foundation.

For any cost study, researchers must determine and clearly define the activities for which resources and expenditures are estimated and define the perspective from which costs are being considered (National Academies of Sciences, Engineering, and Medicine, 2016). Because this report is intended primarily to inform school district activities, the estimates we provide focus specifically on resources and expenditures that school districts bore, although we discuss costs that other organizations, such as institutions of higher education or private funders, covered.

Defining principal pipeline activities and identifying the resources associated with those activities is challenging. Pipeline activities span organizational boundaries within a school district and cut across multiple expenditure categories. Some of the offices expending these resources have responsibility for teachers and other district

---

2 See, for example, Odden et al., 2002, and Miles et al., 2004.

Box 1.1

The Principal Pipeline Initiative

The Principal Pipeline Initiative provided resources to six urban school districts to put in place a pipeline for preparing and supporting novice principals. Each district was expected to align preservice preparation, selective hiring and placement, and support and evaluation with leadership standards (see Figure 1.1). Districts were also expected to develop systems of support to sustain these efforts after the end of the grant period. The Wallace Foundation selected six districts that already viewed school leadership as an important lever for school improvement and that were already using the principal pipeline as a strategic lever for school improvement. The foundation provided resources to these districts in order to catalyze those efforts and develop principal pipelines as defined by the grant. Those districts were

- Charlotte–Mecklenburg Schools, North Carolina
- Denver Public Schools, Colorado
- Gwinnett County Public Schools, Georgia
- Hillsborough County Public Schools, Florida
- New York City Department of Education, New York
- Prince George's County Public Schools, Maryland.

These districts are all large school districts serving students in urban areas. According to the most-recent data from the National Center for Education Statistics (NCES),[a] they are all among the top 50 school districts in the United States in terms of enrollment. As of school year (SY) 2014–2015, at least 10 percent of the student population in each district were English language learners, at least 50 percent received free or reduced-price lunch, and between 64 and 94 percent were not white.

To support this work, The Wallace Foundation initially awarded each district $7.5 million to $12.5 million (see The Wallace Foundation, 2011). The foundation supplemented that initial funding with targeted technical assistance to support structured interactions with preservice preparation providers through Quality Measures (a tool that Education Development Center developed for improving partnerships between school districts and principal preservice preparation providers), the development of leader tracking systems (LTSs), and additional funding of $430,000 to $1 million per district to improve principal supervision (The Wallace Foundation, 2014). Districts also leveraged funding from federal sources (e.g., those under Titles I and II of the Elementary and Secondary Education Act, Race to the Top), state and local sources, and support from foundations to support initiative activities. A series of implementation reports by Policy Studies Associates (PSA), culminating in Turnbull, Anderson, et al., 2016, documented the starting point for each district, as well as the changes each district undertook.[b]

These reports indicated that districts varied in terms of their starting points with respect to each initiative component, as well as areas of intended focus for the initiative. At the same time, each district was able to implement and sustain enhancements to its pipeline and institutionalize features of principal pipelines that research has indicated are critical to success. Notably, each district did the following:

- developed or revised leader standards and utilized those standards to align and guide preservice preparation, selective hiring, and on-the-job support and evaluation
- developed partnerships with principal preservice providers or developed or refined in-house principal preparation programs
- revised principal hiring and placement processes to be informed by more data and aligned with leader standards
- revised principal evaluation processes to align with leader standards and inform development and delivery of on-the-job support
- developed LTSs (see Box 1.2).

In addition, five of the six districts reduced the number of principals that each principal supervisor oversees—or the "span of control"—and reshaped the job of principal supervisors. The districts also worked to improve the quality of preservice preparation options, either developing or improving their own preservice preparation programs or promoting improvement in programs with university or nonprofit partners. Recognizing that these preservice preparation program improvement efforts take several years or more to improve the quality of sitting principals, districts participating in the Principal Pipeline Initiative prioritized efforts described in the bulleted list above (Turnbull, Riley, Arcaira, et al., 2013, Vol. 2, p. 36). Participating districts pursued and continue to pursue their pipeline enhancement work using a continuous quality improvement approach—starting small and learning from preliminary implementation to make adjustments while moving forward (see Turnbull, Anderson, et al., 2016).

[a] See NCES, 2015, and public school data available through the NCES Elementary/Secondary Information System available at NCES, undated (a).

[b] See The Wallace Foundation, undated, for the complete series.

staff, as well as principals. District personnel might not be able to readily identify all the school district staff spending a substantial portion of their time on principal pipeline activities. For this study, we had to make some decisions about what to include as a principal pipeline activity and what to leave out, and we documented those decisions in this report. As ongoing research generates evidence regarding the effects of initiative investments, these estimates of the resources required to operate and enhance principal pipelines can serve as a resource for district decisionmaking about whether certain investments in the principal pipeline are worthwhile.

Box 1.2
Leader Tracking Systems

Each of the participating districts developed an LTS: a database with longitudinal information about current and aspiring principals that would potentially support data-driven decisionmaking regarding principal selection, hiring, and support, as well as meet the data requirements of a rigorous evaluation of the initiative. Developing an LTS required each district to identify all the relevant data sources regarding current and aspiring principals (typically housed in different district offices across the district); address issues with data quality, including critical gaps in the data; compile the data into a usable, longitudinal format; and develop user-friendly systems through which district personnel could access information that would meet their most-pressing needs. To accomplish this work, each district "established cross-departmental teams" (Gill, 2016, p. 3) that included representatives from several different departments, such as human resources (HR), leadership development, talent management, information technology, business applications, and business systems. Several districts also hired outside consultants to assist with the initial information technology systems and database software development while training in-house staff to manage the work in the future. In addition, The Wallace Foundation supported work by a consulting firm—Alvarez and Marsal—to provide guidance on LTS development in each district.

The resulting LTS in each district contained information on educational background, employment history within and outside the district, ratings by teachers, ratings by supervisors, specialized skills of interest to the district, and test scores of students at current and previous schools, as well as other information. The vast majority of district officials in all participating districts indicated that they found the LTS to be worthwhile or very worthwhile, according to an informal survey conducted by The Wallace Foundation (Gill, 2016).

Definition of a Principal Pipeline

After more than a decade of work on school leadership and the surrounding structures that support it, The Wallace Foundation concluded that districtwide principal pipelines could serve as a strategic lever to promote school improvement.[3] The foundation identified four key components of a principal pipeline: (1) leader standards that guide all pipeline activities; (2) preservice preparation opportunities for assistant principals (APs) and principals (including not only the preservice training itself but also recruitment and selection into these opportunities); (3) selective hiring and placement; and

3 For more background on the initiative, see Turnbull, Riley, Arcaira, et al., 2013.

(4) on-the-job induction, evaluation, and support. In addition, school districts must develop the capacity, culture, and infrastructure to sustain the work across components. Figure 1.1 provides a visual description of a comprehensive principal pipeline. The foundation posited that a comprehensive principal pipeline would be more effective than business-as-usual approaches to the preparation and management of school leaders, and it launched the Principal Pipeline Initiative in 2011 to test that hypothesis. Box 1.1 provides an overview of the initiative.

Principal pipeline activities are those activities undertaken by a *district* to prepare, support, manage, and oversee the work of school leaders in order to ensure their effectiveness. Principal pipeline activities include activities that are referred to as principal talent management or human capital management (George W. Bush Institute, 2016). Any district that employs more than a few principals devotes resources to at least some principal pipeline activities even if it does not have in place a comprehensive pipeline as defined by the initiative.

Many education interventions involve introducing a new set of activities to the daily work of schools or districts. The Principal Pipeline Initiative was different. It involved specific enhancements to what the participating districts were doing to manage and support principals. As described in Box 1.1, The Wallace Foundation chose to support the enhancement efforts of districts that were already committed to improving their principal pipelines and had taken some steps toward implementing principal pipelines.

Figure 1.1
Definition of a Comprehensive Principal Pipeline

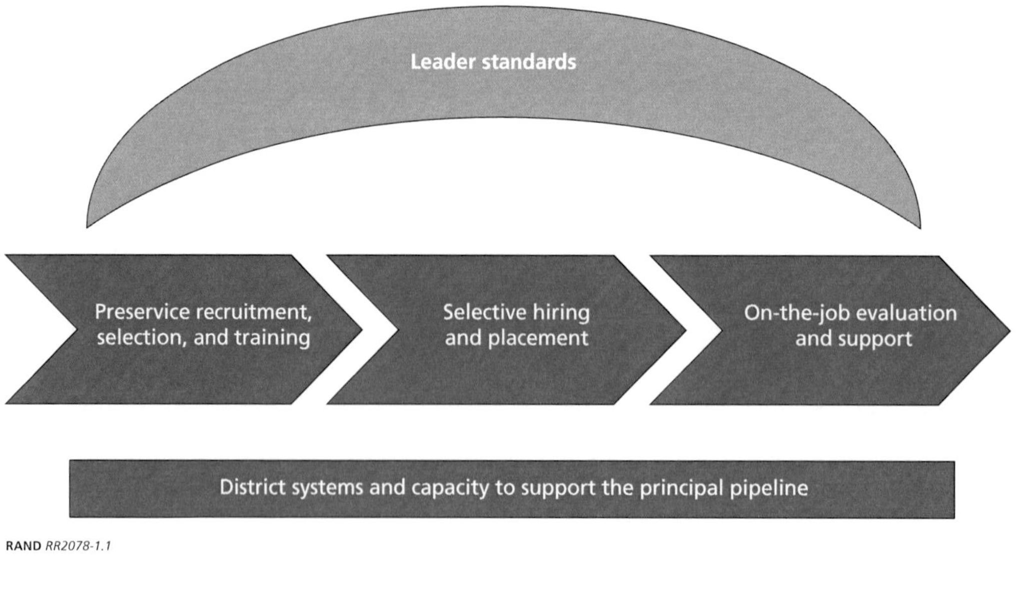

RAND *RR2078-1.1*

The District Role in School Leadership

Although the principal is, at times, described as the chief executive officer of the school (Haberman, 2011), most principals are, in actuality, employees of districts or CMOs. A principal who works in a stand-alone charter school, an independent private school, or a one-school district is responsible for everything that happens in the school and might play a role similar to that of a chief executive officer of a corporation. But a principal working in a district or CMO with several, dozens, or hundreds of schools has a role that could be seen as more equivalent to a line manager in a corporation (see Huselid, Becker, and Beatty, 2005, p. 188). That principal is responsible for executing the district strategy through use of resources provided to the district. This is why the district role in school leadership is so critical. The effectiveness with which the district defines expectations for and manages school leaders will, in turn, influence the effectiveness of those school leaders.

The school district role in school leadership is challenging because principals' work is—in itself—difficult to define. School leaders establish short-term and long-term priorities that influence what they do each day. The school and district contexts influence these priorities. Moreover, school leaders must respond to unanticipated events. For example, when the school goes into lockdown because of an active-shooter incident near the school, the principal's primary focus is to ensure the safety of all students and staff members. Responding to an active-shooter incident might not be written into the principal's job description, but responding effectively is an implicit requirement of the job.

Professional organizations have established standards describing competencies that all school leaders should possess, and most states have established standards for school leadership that guide the approval of preservice programs, state licensure for school leaders, and school leader evaluations. These standards are comprehensive but also quite general because principals' day-to-day activities can vary a great deal, depending on their school context, district expectations, and resources to support school leadership (see Box 1.3).

Investments to Develop Comprehensive Principal Pipelines

The Principal Pipeline Initiative catalyzed districts to make investments in the pipeline systems that support the critically important people who lead or will lead schools. All pipeline activities are intended to improve the quality of the people leading schools and, in particular, the quality of those newly hired into leadership positions. Pipeline districts view all such expenditures (i.e., expenditures devoted to build and operate principal pipelines) as an investment in better leaders and, ultimately, in better schools. The notion that improved leadership can benefit organizations is not unique

Box 1.3

Leader Standards

The National Policy Board for Educational Administration released Professional Standards for Educational Leaders in 2015, updating the Interstate School Leaders Licensure Consortium Standards released in 2008. The standards are intended to inform and shape policy at the state and local levels with regard to preservice preparation, certification, evaluation, and PD of school leaders. The professional standards for school leaders cover ten domains: mission, vision, and core values; ethics and professional norms; equity and cultural responsiveness; curriculum, instruction, and assessment; community of care and support for students; professional capacity of school personnel; professional community for teachers and staff; meaningful engagement of families and community; operations and management; and school improvement.

The standards break down each domain into elements that describe the work required to meet the standards, underscoring the complexity of the principal's role. It is worth noting that "tending to their own learning and effectiveness through reflection, study and improvement, maintaining a healthy work–life balance" is an element of the domain of professional capacity of school personnel, underscoring the fact that school leaders, as well as school districts, are responsible for and bear some costs associated with ensuring effective school leadership.

No school district can anticipate the full range of circumstances that a principal might face in the job and specify actions to be taken under all circumstances. As a result, the contract between a school district and a principal is necessarily incomplete (Williamson, 2002). This implies that the districts must engage in active but flexible oversight of principals. According to Southern Regional Education Board, 2010, highly effective districts delegate responsibility for implementing a school-level strategic plan to the principal and organize the central office to support principals. Districts can also take certain responsibilities off of a principal's plate (and out of the job description) by providing certain supports centrally—freeing up the principal to do other things. For example, many school districts have district specialists who develop (or assist principals in developing) individualized education programs for special needs students or provide (or assist principals in providing) additional support for new teachers. This division of responsibilities between the school and the district varies by district, implying differences in a principal's job by district. This district role in effectively framing and overseeing the employment relationship between districts and school leaders is at the heart of the Principal Pipeline Initiative.

to the initiative or to public education more generally. A 2016 survey of more than 7,000 businesses and HR leaders in more than 130 countries found that leadership is a high-priority issue across countries and sectors. Eighty-nine percent of respondents to that survey reported that improving organizational leadership was an important or very important priority, with more than 50 percent rating leadership as very important (Wakefield et al., 2016, p. 27). Additionally, corporate spending on leadership has been on the increase; studies suggest that high-performing companies spend as much as four times more than their competitors on leadership (Wakefield et al., 2016, p. 28).

Some might view all spending on principal pipelines (both enhancement and operation) as investments in school leaders, schools, and students. However, in this report, we use the term *investment* more narrowly to describe the resources that participating districts devoted to system enhancements, whereas we describe *ongoing costs* as those necessary to support ongoing operations for activities.

It is too early to assess whether these investments have paid off. The implications would be realized only over an extended period of time, with investments in some pipeline categories possibly yielding benefits more quickly than others. But is possible to outline the key potential payoffs from these pipeline investments:

- **Better school leadership could allow schools to be more efficient and effective.** As a result, student outcomes and stakeholder satisfaction could also improve.
- **Lower leadership turnover could reduce future district expenditures on the leadership pipeline, particularly those related to turnover.** The Principal Pipeline Initiative aligns with evidence-based recommendations from the HR management literature for reducing employee turnover (Allen, Bryant, and Vardaman, 2010). Leader standards can promote role clarity and reduce role conflict—things that have been shown to be strongly correlated with turnover (p. 54). The initiative's selective hiring and placement efforts "provide applicants the most comprehensive picture of the organization [and] assess applicant fit with the job and organization"—things that have also been shown to limit turnover (Allen, Bryant, and Vardaman, 2010, p. 56). The initiative's emphasis on early-career mentoring and support, communication of clear expectations and evaluation against those expectations, and high-quality supervision are other recommended approaches for limiting turnover (Allen, Bryant, and Vardaman, 2010, p. 57). By reducing turnover, school districts can avoid turnover costs. The HR literature suggests that turnover costs can be substantial—ranging from 75 to 200 percent of salary costs (Cascio, 2006). Lower turnover could also have implications for future spending on the principal pipeline. Having fewer leadership vacancies because of turnover could lead to reduced district spending on preparation, hiring, and early-career support over time.
- **Having higher-quality school leaders could reduce turnover among the teachers whom they supervise.** Research shows that good bosses enhance the

productivity of the workers they supervise and that those workers are less likely than those with less good bosses to leave an organization (Lazear, Shaw, and Stanton, 2015). This implies that improved school leadership could not only improve teacher effectiveness but also reduce turnover among teachers and the associated costs that districts incur (Burkhauser, 2017; Watlington et al., 2010).

An evaluation of initiative implementation that PSA conducted identified some encouraging signs about the possible value of pipeline investments. Notably, the study found the following:

- Leader standards were a powerful tool for "helping districts align their actions and policies to their priorities for school leadership" (Turnbull, Anderson, et al., 2016, p. 9).
- "[P]olicies and procedures for principal hiring were not hard to change and results were visible in survey responses" (Turnbull, Anderson, et al., 2016, p. 25).
- "[M]ost new principals valued the support from supervisors, mentors and coaches" (Turnbull, Anderson, et al., 2016, p. 37).

As ongoing research generates evidence regarding the effects of initiative investments, the estimates of the resources required to operate and enhance principal pipelines can serve as guidance for district decisionmaking about whether certain investments in the principal pipeline are worthwhile.

Scope

Our study analyzed the costs associated with district principal pipeline efforts in six large urban districts. We provide estimates of how much these districts spent in a baseline, preinitiative SY (2010–2011) and in five SYs that spanned the initiative (2011–2012 through 2015–2016). The preinitiative year provides information on business as usual in these districts. Principal pipelines are potentially relevant in any context in which principals are employed by an organization (a district or a CMO) that is managing many principals. In such a context, the organization has to make strategic choices about how it prepares, manages, and supports school leaders.

Our study provides estimates of the cost of investing in and operating principal pipelines. Because the initiative's effects are not yet known, we cannot link cost estimates to estimates of effectiveness, benefit, or utility as required by cost-effectiveness, cost–benefit, or cost–utility analysis or an analysis of return on investment (Levin and McEwan, 2000; Levenson et al., 2014). As a result, our study does not shed light on whether the initiative is worthwhile from a cost perspective, although it lays the groundwork for such analysis in the future.

The districts in this study are somewhat unusual, in that they are among the 50 largest school districts in the United States. In addition, the participating districts had already committed some resources to strengthening preparation and support for school leaders prior to the initiative. The cost estimates we present might thus be more generalizable to other large districts that view school leadership as a strategic lever for school reform. Nonetheless, many of the lessons we derive from our analysis also provide useful points of reflection for any district that is considering engaging in efforts to prepare, support, and oversee school leaders. In particular, the activities that we have identified as part of a comprehensive principal pipeline could help any district contemplating a principal pipeline.

Overview of This Report

Our study aimed to develop an approach for examining the resources and expenditures that participating districts have devoted to their principal pipelines and applied that framework to generate estimates regarding how much the districts spent on their principal pipelines over the course of the initiative, both overall and for the particular pipeline categories: leader standards, preservice preparation, selective hiring and placement, and on-the-job support and evaluation. We explored both the investments districts made to further develop and revise their principal pipelines and the ongoing costs for maintaining their pipelines over time. We also considered trends in spending over time, including estimates of what districts spent on their principal pipelines prior to the initiative and what they spent as Wallace Foundation funding for the initiative drew to a close.

In Chapter Two, we describe our approach to this study, including information regarding our data collection, what we included in our estimates of pipeline resources and expenditures, and how we derived those estimates from our data sources, as well as the challenges and limitations of our work. Throughout this report, we generally refer to principal pipeline "costs" as those related to our analysis of both the resources—in terms of personnel time—and expenditures necessary to implement a comprehensive principal pipeline in each district. In Chapter Three, we begin by providing estimates of overall average costs across the participating districts for principal pipelines and for each pipeline component. In Chapter Four, we then consider what share of those costs might be considered "investment" costs versus ongoing spending necessary to operate principal pipelines, and we examine how The Wallace Foundation contributed to investment and ongoing costs. We also examine costs of district personnel in greater detail, as well as costs of principal and AP time on pipeline categories. Last, in Chapter Five, we consider key takeaways and implications based on our findings. The appendix provides some of the more-technical details of our data collection and analysis.

CHAPTER TWO

Approach

We designed the approach for this study to provide clear information about the resources and expenditures associated with principal pipeline activities in the six school districts that received funding from The Wallace Foundation through the Principal Pipeline Initiative. This report offers two practical resources to school districts. First, it provides a comprehensive list of activities that could conceivably be part of principal pipelines. This list is not intended to be a prescriptive list of all the activities districts must undertake in order to build comprehensive principal pipelines. Instead, it is intended to help districts understand the range of activities that make up comprehensive principal pipelines in districts participating in the Principal Pipeline Initiative. This list can help other districts assess what they are already doing and identify options for pipeline enhancement. Second, this report provides information about the potential cost to the district of those activities based on the experience of participating districts. To that end, we provide average annual costs during the main SYs of the initiative (2011–2012 to 2014–2015), as well as costs over time for major initiative activity categories.

In presenting the cost information, we focus attention on two issues of particular interest to districts. First, we look at how much of that total district cost is due to the salary cost of district personnel versus other expenditures (e.g., materials, hardware, software, consultants). The time that personnel spend on pipeline activities will take time away from other activities and priorities, and we describe the cost of that time to help districts consider strategies for restructuring positions and staff, depending on what elements of their pipelines they wish to develop or enhance. Secondly, to underscore the fact that ongoing costs are associated with operating principal pipelines even after investments are made to build those pipelines, we provide estimates for the costs of one-time investments to principal pipelines versus the ongoing costs that are expected to repeat over time.

We begin this chapter with further description of our activity-based approach and present the list of key activities that we identified as part of a comprehensive pipeline in participating districts. We then discuss what we included in and excluded from our cost estimates, based on our aims and available data. We then provide additional information regarding our data collection, including our data sources and methods, followed by a discussion of key analyses.

Activities Associated with a Comprehensive Principal Pipeline

We used an activity-based approach in our data-gathering and analysis.[1] Similar methods have been used to characterize school district expenditures on teacher PD (see Miles et al., 2004, and Chambers, Lam, and Mahitivanichcha, 2008). Following this approach, we first developed a list of activities that could be associated with principal pipelines.[2] As noted in Chapter One, we intended this activity list to encompass the *school district's* work to support, manage, and oversee its principal pipeline. We did not intend for it to include the work that *principals themselves* do on a daily basis as part of their school leadership roles. We categorized each activity under one of the four categories of a comprehensive pipeline as already described in this report: leader standards; preservice recruitment, selection, and preparation; selective hiring and placement; and on-the-job support and evaluation. We also gathered information on systems of support for the principal pipeline, which made up a fifth category of activities for our analysis.

We identified these activities through an iterative approach, starting with expenditures included in the districts' expenditure reports to The Wallace Foundation. We mapped those expenditures into activities, and we vetted our activity list with district contacts and the foundation, updating the activity list based on their feedback. When an activity was particularly complex (e.g., districts pursued different approaches to the activity or the activity was different for principals and APs), we divided that activity into *subactivities*. We refined the major activities and subactivities through an iterative process of coding reported expenditures within each district and then gleaning additional information on reported and unreported expenditures through interviews with district personnel engaged in each activity.[3]

Table 2.1 provides the resulting list of activities and subactivities. We have noted activities and subactivities for which we placed principal and AP resources and expenditures in two separate categories so that we could examine these costs separately (although we generally decided to combine principal and AP costs in our reporting).

In components 2 and 4, some of the main activities and subactivities reflect whether the activity's or subactivity's target was principals or APs.[4] In addition, some

---

[1] See, for example, the activity-based costing framework outlined in Kaplan and Cooper, 1998.

[2] In the cost study literature, these activities are referred to as *cost ingredients*. See Levin and McEwan, 2000. It should be noted that Levin and McEwan recommend applying a cost ingredient approach to capture the full social cost of an intervention. As discussed, our study takes a more limited view, estimating costs from the district's perspective and thus omitting some pipeline costs that other stakeholders might incur.

[3] Qualitative coding processes like the ones we used for this work are described in detail in, for example, Strauss and Corbin, 1998, and Lincoln and Guba, 1985.

[4] Even if APs are the focus of a particular activity, that activity could ultimately be viewed as principal preparation. Prior research emphasizes the assistant principalship as a key step to the principalship in participating districts (Turnbull, Riley, and MacFarlane, 2015).

preservice preparation programs were in-house programs that the districts delivered, whereas other programs were provided at higher education institutions in partnership with districts. Thus, we broke the main activity of preservice preparation program delivery into four subactivities: internal district preservice to prepare principals, internal district preservice to prepare APs, external preservice to prepare principals, and external preservice to prepare APs.

Some of the other activities and subactivities listed in the table require elaboration. Quality Measures is a tool that Education Development Center developed for improving partnerships between school districts and principal preservice providers. School Administration Manager (SAM) is a daily PD set of practices designed to help leaders increase time spent on instructional leadership activities and reflect on impact and next steps. The National SAM Innovation Project, a nonprofit organization, provides SAM services to schools, districts, and states. Vanderbilt Assessment of Leadership in Education (VAL-ED) is a principal-evaluation tool for assessing principal behaviors. The Wallace Foundation supported the development of all three tools—Quality Measures, SAM and VAL-ED—prior to the launch of the initiative. The Wallace Foundation required all participating districts to use Quality Measures during the initiative, and all districts did. The foundation also required participating districts to use behavioral assessment to evaluate principals. Four of the six participating districts chose to use VAL-ED for this purpose. Districts were introduced to the SAM process. The National SAM Innovation Project requires that principal and district leader participation be voluntary. All six districts elected to offer the SAM process to select school leaders. We listed these as subactivities so that we could explore spending on principal pipelines with and without these tools and approaches. In describing our findings, we combined the costs associated with these specific activities with the broader, related category of activities.

We developed our principal pipeline activity list through an examination of all resources and expenditures that participating districts devoted to principal pipelines. Not every participating district engaged in every subactivity or activity, and other school districts might be engaged in principal pipeline–related activities that are not reflected here. However, this activity list does reflect key principal pipeline activities in districts that were deeply engaged in supporting and improving their pipelines, so the list represents a fairly comprehensive illustration of the possible activities that other districts could implement and improve in order to strengthen their principal pipelines. This list of activities guided our data-collection and analysis process, which we describe in more detail in the next section. The activity list itself can also serve as a practical resource to other districts by helping them identify what pieces of their principal pipelines are already in place in their districts and what additional activities they might consider undertaking in their contexts.

Table 2.1
Principal Pipeline Activities and Subactivities, by Major Category

Category	Component	Activity	Subactivity
Pipeline component	1. Leader standards	Develop or revise leader standards and secure their approval.	—
	2. Preservice preparation	Revise the system of preservice preparation.	Develop internal, district-led preservice courses.[a] Develop external program or university-based courses.[a] Develop screening and selection processes.[a] Prepare and train personnel to use the new screening and selection processes.
		Recruit principal and AP candidates for preservice preparation.	—
		Screen and select candidates for preservice preparation.[a]	—
		Deliver preservice preparation.	Deliver internal, district-led preparation.[a] Deliver external contractor- or partner-led preparation.[a]
		Oversee the quality of the portfolio of preservice preparation programs.	Conduct a Quality Measures review.[b] Oversee the quality of preservice preparation (beyond Quality Measures).
	3. Selective hiring and placement	Revise the system for principal recruiting, hiring, and placement (design processes and train personnel).	—
		Recruit principal and AP candidates.	—
		Screen, select, and support the candidate pool.[a]	—
		Interview and hire school leaders.[a]	—

Table 2.1—Continued

Category	Component	Activity	Subactivity
	4. On-the-job support and evaluation	Revise the system for providing on-the-job support and evaluation for principals and APs.	Design new on-the-job support and induction processes and courses and provide personnel training. Design new evaluation processes, including technology, and provide personnel training.
		Provide on-the-job support and induction for principals and APs.	Provide induction and first-year on-the-job PD.[a] Provide on-the-job PD after the first year.[a] Provide schoolwide support via teams and networks. Support the implementation of SAM.[b]
		Evaluate principals and APs.	Evaluate principals and APs aside from the use of VAL-ED.[c] Evaluate principals using VAL-ED.
		Provide executive coaching and support to those who supervise and support principals.	—
Systems and capacity for supporting the pipeline components		Revise the overall principal pipeline.	—
		Develop and disseminate communication about the initiative.	—
		Develop and maintain an LTS.	—
		Oversee implementation of the pipeline (quality assurance).	—

[a] Separate activity or subactivity for principals and for APs.

[b] SAM is a daily PD set of practices designed to help leaders increase time spent on instructional leadership activities and reflect on impact and next steps. The National SAM Innovation Project developed it with support from The Wallace Foundation.

[c] VAL-ED is a principal-evaluation tool for assessing principal behaviors. Vanderbilt University developed it with support from The Wallace Foundation.

What We Included in and Excluded from Our Estimates

As with any cost study, we had to make decisions about what to include in and exclude from our cost estimates. Table 2.2 provides an overview of those decisions, which we also describe in more detail below, along with the associated challenges and limitations that each decision presented.

Inclusion of Costs That School Districts Bore

Because this study strived to provide school districts with clear information about district costs for developing and maintaining principal pipelines, our accounting focused on the costs borne by the district and not exhaustive costs borne by other stakeholders, including outside organizations, consultants, contractors, and aspiring or current leaders themselves. For example, in accounting for the costs associated with an external preservice preparation program, we accounted for the personnel time that the district incurred in partnering with an external program, and we accounted for any subcontract expenditures with that preservice preparation program provider. However, we did not account for the time that external consultants might have spent on such a program beyond what was reported in subcontracts or consultant agreements. We accounted only for the documented expense of a vendor's activities to the district; we did not account for any profit or loss to the vendor, nor did we account for philanthropic, public, or endowment funds that might be used to supplement the revenue that the vendor receives from the district. We took into account district expenditures for pipeline activities funded through The Wallace Foundation's investments, as well as costs funded through any other source, including district funds.

Table 2.2
Costs Included in and Excluded from Our Estimates

Included	Excluded
• Costs borne by school districts themselves, including cost of personnel time and ODCs (e.g., materials, software) • Costs of work funded through both The Wallace Foundation and other funding sources • Costs of time for district personnel who supported principal pipeline efforts, including those across multiple offices (e.g., HR, leadership, information technology) • Costs of schoolwide supports that also provided direct and explicit support to principals • Costs for technology that supported the pipeline (e.g., hardware and software necessary for LTSs)	• Costs that outside consultants or subcontracts bore beyond what the district paid for those services • Costs of time for principals and APs who took part in pipeline activities (excluding payments to those supporting the pipeline on top of salaries) • Opportunity costs of district personnel time, beyond estimates for the cost of personnel time for individual activities • Costs of schoolwide supports that did not explicitly support principals • New York City resources and expenditures for two major categories for which data were unavailable: (1) selective hiring and placement and (2) on-the-job support and evaluation

NOTE: ODC = other direct cost.

Our estimates regarding the costs of specific activities included both the time of district personnel who directed or supported those activities and the nonpersonnel costs for expenditures related to contracted services, technology, materials, supplies, travel, or any other costs that the district paid for those activities. *However, we did not include costs for the time that principals and APs invested in particular principal pipeline activities unless those principals or APs received supplemental stipends or payments beyond their regular salaries for that time or in the rare case that someone was explicitly assigned as a substitute for an administrator who was participating in a pipeline activity and was therefore out of the building.* We also excluded time or out-of-pocket costs that people incurred to participate in preservice programs, PD, or mentoring of others.

Challenges of Accounting for District Personnel Time

No single office or department in a school district handles all aspects of the principal pipeline. An important step in identifying key pipeline personnel was building a shared understanding with the districts about the activities included in a principal pipeline. After districts understood what we were including as part of the principal pipeline, they were better able to direct us to all the offices and departments doing pipeline-related work. Through discussion with those who directed or managed particular aspects of the pipeline, we then worked with districts to identify all the personnel who spent substantial portions of their time (i.e., 5 percent or more of all their district work) on principal pipelines. Those few district personnel who had a bird's-eye view of the pipeline could usually direct us to the district offices or departments that handled hiring, placement, PD support, and evaluation. Such offices include the obvious ones, such as those focused on HR, school support, and principal supervision. But they also included offices and departments that maintain the information technology that supports personnel hiring, support, and supervision; budget offices that oversee spending and initiatives related to principals; or offices housing administrative support personnel who might help with, for example, registration of principals for PD programs or planning (e.g., ordering coffee, food) for screening and hiring events. But occasionally, in larger districts, even personnel leading the initiative work might not be aware of some activities or new funding for programs that affect the pipeline. Even in a district with a single department or office that handles leadership-related work, at least a handful of other offices are involved with the principal pipeline in some way. It is possible that we did not count the time of at least some personnel who do contribute some portion of their time to principal pipeline activities.

One limitation of our personnel cost estimates is that self-reported estimates of time and percentage of effort on pipeline activities are inevitably imprecise, particularly given that some of these data were gathered retrospectively (e.g., personnel data and preinitiative expenditures). We received initial estimates of personnel time on pipeline activities through our main district point of contact, who typically managed, coordinated, and oversaw all staff who spent time on pipeline activities. We then confirmed those time estimates with individual personnel who did that work or managed others who did that work. One issue was that personnel with whom we spoke often found it challenging to provide percentage of time estimates even for more-recent time periods, given that so much of their work is intertwined and cross-cutting. The goal of our cost study was to understand approximate costs of principal pipelines and the relative costs of the activities that are part of that pipeline.

Exclusion of Opportunity Costs for Personnel Time

Even though we accounted for the time that district central office staff reported spending on various activities and included that in the cost of those activities, our estimates might not fully capture the costs of those activities. Specifically, all district staff members have limited time available. Therefore, time that staff spent on pipeline activities has *opportunity costs* associated with it. Opportunity costs are defined as "benefit[s] that a person could have received, but gave up, to take another course of action" ("Opportunity Cost," undated). As described in Levin and McEwan, 2000, "[b]y using resources in one way, we are giving up the ability to use them in another way, so a cost has been incurred" (p. 44). For example, when a principal is pulled out of school for a day to participate in hiring pool screening, that principal is not in the school building supporting teachers and students. The value of what the principal would have been doing in the school that day is the opportunity cost of that principal's participation in the hiring pool.[5] The concept of opportunity cost also applies to the time of central office personnel. If the superintendent participates in a leader standards development committee, that superintendent is spending less (or no) time on other initiatives or programs. We discuss this opportunity cost as part of our report, but we do not directly account for it other than accounting for the cost of personnel time on particular activities. As noted, Table 2.2 provides additional information about key principal pipeline costs that we included in our study and what we did not include as part of our estimates.

As a separate input to guide district decisionmaking, we do provide information about principal and AP reports of the time and money that they invested in various activities. Specifically, we present some information on average costs of the principal pipeline to principals and APs based on a survey of novice principals and APs in their first three years on the job in each district. These data have some limitations, given that they include only novice leaders. But they do include information about costs that all school leaders might be expected to invest at some point in their careers, including average out-of-pocket costs for preservice leadership preparation, as well as investments of time in various aspects of the principal pipeline, including hiring of new leaders and coaching or mentoring new leaders. These data give districts a picture of the opportunity costs associated with principal and AP time devoted to pipeline activities.

[5] It is worth noting that school districts rarely provide substitutes when administrators are absent.

Inclusion of Schoolwide Support That Districts Provided

A key challenge with which we grappled during this study was when to account for schoolwide support that a district provided to individual schools. Variation in these supports reflects variation across districts in the way in which they allocate responsibilities to the district central office versus the school. Larger districts organize some types of specialized support in centralized offices and deploy that support to schools. Some of that support (e.g., principal coaching and mentoring) is focused directly on school leaders. But much of that centralized support targets teachers or students and is not specifically intended to support school leadership. For example, special needs coordinators, support teams for novice teachers, or math specialists would typically work directly with teachers or students. District decisions about supports provided through district central offices influence the scope of the principal's job. For example, a behavioral support specialist might provide demonstrations for and coach teachers who are struggling with classroom management—something a principal might spend time doing if those district supports were not available.

Through interviews conducted at the start of this project, we realized that districts participating in the Principal Pipeline Initiative took dramatically different approaches to providing and accounting for provision of school support. In some cases, districts shifted their approaches to school support during the initiative. For this study, we had to make a choice about where to draw the line between school supports and principal supports. We chose to draw that line in a very conservative way. Although we agreed that "schoolwide support via teams and networks" is one activity that is part of the on-the-job support and evaluation component of the principal pipeline, we counted support as support for the principal only if the support was directly targeting the principal and that principal's skills or PD. By this measure, an executive coach for principals is clearly included, but the aforementioned behavioral specialist or a community-relations liaison is excluded, even if that person's support takes some responsibility off of the principal's plate. We acknowledge that the level of schoolwide supports that a district provides to the school will have implications for principal workload and, ultimately, principal effectiveness. And there might be trade-offs between the level of schoolwide support provided and principal support needed. In other words, a district that provides little schoolwide support might provide substantially more support for principals.[6] In addition, districts might organize these school supports differently and allocate different levels of resources to them. Our estimates might be capturing principal supports that some districts provide that are similar to school supports that are not captured in other districts.

---

[6] For a useful overview of how shifts in support for principals can influence overall school funding, see G. Johnson, 2014.

Inclusion of Data from New York City

One additional issue was that some data in regard to costs for all major categories of principal pipeline activities in New York City were not available. In New York City, schools are managed by a citywide department rather than a school district per se. As a result, New York City Department of Education (DOE) budgetary and expenditure information is housed in many different offices and in many different forms. Furthermore, how principal supervisors spend their time and support principals is extremely variable in New York City and dependent on specific guidelines and choices in individual districts in the New York City DOE. For these reasons, we include the New York City DOE in our average calculations only for the major categories for which we could get reasonable comprehensive estimates of costs from the New York City DOE Office of Leadership. Those categories are component 1 (leader standards) and component 2 (preservice preparation), as well as systems and capacity for supporting pipeline components. Given that we lack complete information on New York City's spending related to all pipeline activities, we also exclude the city from reports on average costs for all pipeline categories across participating districts.

Accounting for Technology Costs

Beyond the time investment of personnel, other direct costs (ODCs) are involved in supporting the principal pipeline. One direct cost that might not be immediately evident is the cost of the technology supporting the pipeline. The Wallace Foundation encouraged all participating districts to create LTSs that utilized existing and new information systems and technology to help districts systematically collect data on potential and current leaders. An LTS draws on multiple existing data systems—notably, HR data systems. We did not include the costs of these existing, underlying data systems in our estimates. We did include the costs involved in figuring out what data resources are available, aligning different data systems, and developing new visualization tools focused on pipeline issues (Gill, 2016).

Despite these challenges and caveats, our cost estimates provide an overview of the key principal pipeline activities with associated costs and average approximate spending for these activities overall and over time in the six participating districts. As a result, our work provides a unique look at what it takes to build and maintain principal pipelines in large urban districts that have already invested some thought and time in developing their pipelines. Even small districts without similarly developed principal pipelines can glean useful information on major categories of pipeline activities and potential resources and expenditures necessary to upgrade particular pieces of their pipelines.

Data Sources

Principal pipeline costs are not a line item in school budget and expenditure reports. For our cost study, we gathered information about the costs of activities through multiple data sources. We strived to capture all expenditures and personnel resources associated with principal pipelines that a district incurred, regardless of what funding sources the district used to cover them. The data sources for our study included the following:

- **District principal pipeline expenditure reports.** Each participating district provided regular expenditure reports to The Wallace Foundation on its principal pipeline–related spending over the course of the initiative—from August 2011 through December 2015—on all spending on their principal pipelines, including both Wallace and non-Wallace resources.
- **Expenditure reports for technical assistance.** The Wallace Foundation also collected expenditure reports from consultants and organizations with which they contracted to provide guidance to districts for aspects of the Principal Pipeline Initiative, which we used to identify technical assistance work key to districts' pipeline work.
- **In-depth interviews with district personnel.** We conducted numerous interviews with district personnel who managed or played key roles in the initiative to gather more information about costs from the expenditure reports and gaps in initiative expenditures—as we defined them—that might not have been reported in expenditure reports to The Wallace Foundation.
- **District personnel resource-allocation data.** We developed a separate tool to gather data from the district on all the staff involved in principal pipeline activities, the percentage of their time spent on the pipeline over the course of the year, the specific activities on which they focused, and their annual salaries and benefits.
- **Survey data.** PSA and RAND collaborated to administer a survey to all novice principals and APs who had been in their roles for three years or less. We administered the survey in 2014 and 2015. The survey asked these novice principals and APs to estimate the percentage of time they spent on specific pipeline activities, including their own PD and formal mentoring of other school leaders. The survey also asked principals and APs for their agreement about whether their time on pipeline activities supported or hindered their work on other important school priorities. Last, the survey included a question to school leaders about how much they paid out of pocket for their own leadership preparation. More information about the survey is available in Turnbull, Anderson, et al., 2016, Appendix A.[7]

---

[7] The response rates for the survey were relatively high in both 2014 and 2015. As reported in Turnbull, Anderson, et al., 2016, the number of novice principals across participating districts who responded to the survey was 541 in 2014 and 514 in 2015, for average response rates of, respectively, 66 and 65 percent. The number of

Capturing and Categorizing Data Through Our Data-Collection Tools

To facilitate data collection of all resources and expenditures devoted to principal pipelines, we developed a tool for gathering personnel costs and a tool for categorizing all expenditures. Our activity list served as a facilitation tool as well. Specifically, the list prompted districts to consider the full range of resources devoted to an activity. For example, the activity of providing PD to school leaders could include time from any district personnel involved in registering, planning, and delivering a PD event for principals or APs; payments to any external consultants delivering the preparation; costs of materials, supplies, or food or any ODCs for the preparation; cost of any facilities rented for the preparation; and stipends to those attending the preparation (if provided).

The activity list also enabled district personnel to indicate the activities on which they spent their time so that we could estimate the personnel "cost" for those activities. We provide a little more detail in this section on the content of our tools; the appendix also includes snapshots of those tools. Despite our work with districts to identify any resources and expenditures related to each pipeline activity, districts might have differed in their interpretations of what costs were included as part of particular pipeline activities. Thus, we might have missed some pipeline costs for some districts in our data-gathering work.

Personnel Data-Collection Tool

Although expenditure reports that districts provided to The Wallace Foundation were an excellent resource for our study, we realized early on that those reports did not always include information on costs associated with everyone across all district offices who was contributing to the pipeline activities we had identified. For example, to develop a robust LTS, a district must draw on expertise and time from people in multiple district departments, including HR, leadership and supervision, and information technology. Districts might neglect to include all those people in their reporting to The Wallace Foundation because they were not part of the office or department that was leading the initiative. For this reason, we queried districts extensively in interviews about all district staff spending time on any activities on our cost activity list. We created a tool in which districts could provide all the information necessary for us to estimate costs of personnel time on particular pipeline activities, including lists of people spending time on pipeline activities, their salary data, fringe benefit rates, and rough estimates of the proportion of time staff spent on pipeline activities. We then allocated each district staff member's salary and fringe benefit costs to principal pipeline activi-

novice APs who responded to the survey was 671 in 2014 and 688 in 2015, for response rates of, respectively, 73 and 68 percent. When we excluded New York City from the response rate calculations, the average response rates were more than 85 percent in each year for both principals and APs.

ties based on estimates about the proportion of time that staff member spent on each of those activities.

Activity Categorization Tool

Our activity categorization tool was where we entered information about each pipeline expenditure. We entered initial information and categorizations for each expenditure gleaned from our data sources into the tool. We then shared that tool with district points of contact so that they could provide feedback on how we categorized the data and respond to any of our specific questions about those categorizations. The activity categorization tool thus enabled us to keep school districts informed about all the costs we were recording for each pipeline activity over time, and it allowed us to vet the data through multiple rounds of interaction with the districts to ensure accuracy.

When entering data into our tool, we categorized costs as follows:

- **By activity and subactivity.** We associated resources and expenditures with individual pipeline activities in our activity categorization tool. For example, an expenditure for materials or supplies for a district preservice preparation event for principals would be coded under the activity "internal, district-led preparation for principals," whereas the cost of personnel time on the development of a strategy for providing PD to APs would be coded under the activity "revise the system for providing on-the-job support for APs." Sometimes, because staff could not account for their time with such specificity, we coded personnel time into main activities rather than subactivities. Districts confirmed our coding of expenditures by activity and subactivity.
- **By year.** We determined the SY in which a cost occurred, from the start of the initiative through the first six months of 2015–2016.[8] We also gathered retrospective rough estimates of pipeline expenditures from 2010–2011, to which we refer in this report as preinitiative costs.[9]

---

[8] Data sources for this report provided expenditure data through December 31, 2015. Our 2015–2016 estimates are thus projected estimates based on the first six months of expenditures (through December 2015).

[9] Preinitiative costs are very rough estimates of 2010–2011 costs. We used interview data and data from the district proposals to The Wallace Foundation for the initiative to identify activities that occurred in 2011–2012 and that we know also occurred in 2010–2011. In the case of nonpersonnel expenditures (e.g., subcontracts, consultants, ODCs for materials), for those costs we knew had occurred in both years, we simply took the amount for each expenditure reported for 2011–2012 and repeated the cost in 2010–2011. In the case of district personnel expenditures, we estimated costs similarly to how we accounted for personnel time in 2011–2012 and beyond: We retrieved salary and benefit data for personnel whom we knew were working on principal pipeline activities in 2010–2011, allocated their salaries according the percentage of total time that they spent on the pipeline, and divided their percentage time among various pipeline activities that we knew had occurred in 2010–2011. We asked district points of contact to verify our judgments about the 2010–2011 principal pipeline expenditures. We did not categorize preinitiative costs as investment or ongoing because we lacked sufficient information to make those judgments. Because we based preinitiative costs on estimates rather than actual expenditure data, readers should be cautious in drawing interpretations or implications based on preinitiative information.

- **By investments and ongoing.** We coded resources and expenditures according to whether they represented investments or pilot tests that would be expected to take place over only a limited time (e.g., a few years) or ongoing costs that would be expected to repeat for the foreseeable future as the costs of maintaining activities or efforts. For example, the initial delivery of a PD course or program could require one-time development costs that would not be incurred if the program or course were delivered in future years.[10] Districts made judgments about whether a nonpersonnel cost was an investment or ongoing. Personnel costs were determined as investment or ongoing costs based on activity; we classified the costs of personnel time on certain activities as both investment and ongoing costs (e.g., personnel time on development of leader standards), whereas we classified the costs of personnel time on other activities just as ongoing costs (e.g., personnel time to provide on-the-job support).[11]
- **By cost type.** We coded expenditures according to their cost type. Cost types included costs for district personnel (e.g., personnel salary costs or stipends provided to personnel); costs for consultants or subcontracts; and ODCs, such as materials and supplies. In discussing our findings in this report, we distinguish between expenditures related to the time of district personnel and other types of costs, such as materials and consultants.

Categorizing expenditures in these ways supported various types of analyses, including, for example, analyses of trends of change in initiative expenditures over time, differences in personnel and nonpersonnel costs over time, and differences in investment and ongoing costs for each year of the initiative. In the next section, we provide an overview of our analysis and how we used the analysis to address each of our research questions.

Analyzing the Data

We used the activity categorization tool to generate district-by-district summaries of pipeline resources and expenditures. These summary tables included total costs for each activity overall, as well as costs for each year, beginning with the preinitiative SY (2010–2011), continuing through 2014–2015, and including estimates for the first half of 2015–2016. The summary tables also included costs for personnel only, investment costs, and ongoing costs overall and by year.

---

[10] We did discuss with districts the time frame in which they expected to conduct certain activities again, which would have been a time frame over which they might amortize these investment activities. Districts could not provide accurate estimates of this time frame. However, depreciating the costs of these investments over time would have accounted for cost in a way that is more consistent with standard cost methodology.

[11] The appendix contains more details on how we determined investment and ongoing costs for personnel.

We transformed these summary data to account for regional variation in purchasing power (i.e., cost of living) and inflation during the time period. To make these adjustments, we first identified regional price parities (RPPs) for each year from 2010 to 2014 for the metropolitan statistical area (MSA) in which each district was located.[12] RPPs measure the differences in the price levels of goods and services across metropolitan areas for a given year. We used the RPPs for each district's MSA to adjust dollar amounts for each year of our initiative expenditure data. To make the adjustment, we simply divided the costs by the RPP adjustment factor for that year; the RPP adjustment factor for a particular region is the RPP index for that region divided by 100. So, for example, if the RPP adjustment factor for a particular school district geographical area is 95.9 percent in a particular year—meaning that the average price level for that geographical area is just more than 4 percent lower, on average, than other areas—each dollar spent on the initiative in that school district in that year is worth $1.04. To adjust the cost estimates for inflation, we used the Consumer Price Index for All Urban Consumers (CPI-U) to inflate expenditures from earlier years of the initiative to equivalent dollars for the 2015–2016 SY.[13] As a result of these adjustments, costs are reported in terms of real dollar expenditures for the 2015–2016 SY for an average MSA.

Even after making the adjustments for regional variation in purchasing power and inflation, districts varied dramatically in terms of dollars spent. Each pipeline activity is likely to have a fixed and variable cost aspect associated with it. A fixed cost aspect is one that does not vary based on the size of the district or the number of people in the pipeline. For example, the development of LTSs could potentially require a basic level of effort regardless of the size of the district. A variable cost aspect is one that does vary directly based on the size of the district or the number of people participating in or served by a particular activity. Most activities have both fixed and variable costs associated with them, although the relative importance of the two will vary by activity.

Cost drivers are those things that could influence variable costs. In this report, we present cross-district averages in terms of average annual expenditures by some potential cost drivers that would be appropriate to all categories and to which other districts might relate. These are the total number of principals in the district, the number of

---

[12] The RPP index indicates whether the costs of goods and services for a particular MSA are higher or lower than the national average. The index pegs the national average cost of goods and services at 100. Areas where the costs of goods and services are above the national average have indexes above 100; areas where the costs are below the national average have indexes below 100. At the time of this writing, RPPs were available from the Bureau of Economic Analysis through 2014 (Bureau of Economic Analysis, undated). For each SY, we applied the relevant RPP for the first part of that SY (i.e., for the 2010–2011 SY, we used 2010 RPPs). There was not much variation in RPP indexes during this time period. For 2015–2016, we applied the 2014 RPP rate.

[13] Specifically, we used the U.S. city average, a semiannual average for the second half of the calendar year corresponding to the fall semester of the relevant SY. We created an adjustment factor for year *x* by dividing the relevant CPI-U index for 2015 by the relevant CPI-U index for year *x*. We then multiplied our cost estimates for year *x* by that cost factor.

pupils, and average current expenditures per pupil (per-pupil cost).[14] The number of principals is a potential cost driver because the pipeline supports principals directly; each additional principal in the district places more demands on the pipeline as a whole—more principals to be trained, hired, evaluated, and supported. For some pipeline categories and activities, a subset of principals could potentially be a more direct cost driver. For example, the number of principals hired in a particular SY would directly influence the hiring costs for that SY. The number of people participating in preservice preparation could influence the cost of preservice delivery. Where relevant, we did analyze data with regard to other cost drivers and comment on relevant findings. However, use of a common cost driver, such as cost per principal, facilitates comparison across all main categories of pipeline activities. Presenting costs on a per-principal basis also helps districts understand the resources needed to maintain a cadre of principals; per-principal costs might be relevant for district planning because the number of principals is more stable and predictable than the number of vacancies and characteristics of new hires.

The number of pupils is another useful cost driver to consider. Assessing pipeline spending in terms of cost per pupil might account for variation in average school size for which estimates of per-principal spending do not necessarily account. Principals in districts that have larger schools might need additional supports to accomplish the same job. Another advantage of the per-pupil expenditure metric is that it allows for comparison with expenditures on initiatives that have nothing to do with principals. Average current expenditures per pupil, to which we refer as average per-pupil cost, is another useful cost driver because it reflects aspects of the local context that might lead a district to spend more in order to meet the needs of its students than other districts because of either different values and objectives or different community needs.[15]

Table 2.3 summarizes some of these key drivers of total resources and expenditures on principal pipelines in each district. New York City is substantially larger than the other districts in terms of the number of pupils, number of principals, and per-pupil spending. The other districts serve between 78,000 and 213,000 students (depending on the SY) and have between 130 and 276 principals. Table 2.3 suggests that most of the pipeline districts have experienced growth in the number of pupils served during the initiative's time frame and in the number of principals. We did not have complete

---

[14] In this study, cost drivers are an attempt to capture a very general notion of variable costs. Many cost studies distinguish between fixed and variable costs. Fixed costs are those incurred regardless of the number of units produced. Variable costs are those costs that vary depending on how many units are produced. The challenge with using the concept of fixed and variable costs in this study is that the relevant "unit" of analysis differs depending on the subactivity. For example, for preservice delivery, the relevant unit is the number of program participants at a particular point in time. For hiring processes, the relevant unit might be the total number of new hires.

[15] We calculated the average current expenditures per pupil for each district by dividing the total current expenditures (excluding capital improvements and interest on debt) by the total number of pupils as reported in NCES, undated (b).

information on the number of APs for every district and for every year and therefore could not use the number of principals and APs combined as a cost driver. According to available data for SY 2014–2015, Charlotte, Hillsborough, and Prince George's County have between 1.6 and 1.8 APs for each principal. Gwinnett has substantially more APs per principal (3.8 APs for each principal). As can be inferred from Table 2.3, Gwinnett also has more pupils per principal, suggesting a larger average school. Denver has at least 1.1 APs per principal. In Denver, principals have autonomy to use school-level funding to hire APs who might not be recorded in district figures. After adjusting for cost of living, we also adjusted costs in each district depending on various drivers, and we present costs by some cost drivers throughout this report, focusing particularly on cost per principal.

To calculate annual average spending, we took the average of the costs over a particular time span (generally 2011–2012 through 2014–2015) for each district and then calculated the average across districts by adding up those average annual costs and dividing by 6. Because we did not include New York City in the average calculations for components 3 and 4, we divided the summed annual average costs by 5 for those pipeline categories. When we present costs by year, they represent a calculation of average cross-district costs in the same way—by summing the district-by-district costs and dividing by the total number of districts that we summed together.

Because we had only six months' worth of data for SY 2015–2016, we had to extrapolate those data to develop an estimate of resources and expenditures for the entire SY. In addition, expenditures that districts reported for the first six months of 2015–2016 might not be a clear signal of spending across the whole year, given that The Wallace Foundation's funding for the initiative was ending. For example, some districts could have spent more in the first six months of 2015–2016 because they had more funding to support their principal pipelines during that period than they expected to have for the last six months of 2015–2016. We thus have less confidence in our estimates for 2015–2016 and did not include them in our estimates of average annual costs over the entire initiative. We did, however, refer to these extrapolations when describing changes in annual resources and expenditures over time. We used two different sets of assumptions to estimate costs for the entire 2015–2016 SY, and we present a predicted range for pipeline costs based on these different assumptions. We calculated the upper bound or maximum predicted annual costs for 2015–2016 as twice the amount of observed costs for the first half of 2015–2016. The lower bound or minimum predicted annual costs doubled the observed costs for personnel only. The latter approach assumes that the personnel contributed to each pipeline activity over the course of 2015–2016 but that nonpersonnel pipeline costs were front-loaded into the first part of the SY.

In summary, our study approach was particularly intended to provide information to other school districts and those who support districts about what it could take to build a strong principal pipeline. Our report offers two types of practical resources

Table 2.3
Key Cost Drivers in Each District, by School Year

District	Driver	2010–2011	2011–2012	2012–2013	2013–2014	2014–2015	2015–2016
Charlotte	Pupils	134,598	137,016	140,161	142,389	144,497	145,444
	Principals	178	159	159	160	164	168
	Per-pupil expenditures, in dollars	8,628	8,365	8,716	8,906		
Denver	Pupils	78,317	80,890	83,377	86,043	88,839	90,234
	Principals	130	142	148	144	152	157
	Per-pupil expenditures, in dollars	10,075	9,678	9,683	10,138	10,090	
Hillsborough	Pupils	194,528	198,164	200,427	205,743	212,915	
	Principals	241	254	267	271	276	
	Per-pupil expenditures, in dollars	8,770	8,318	8,191	8,659	8,676	
Gwinnett	Pupils	160,744	162,370	164,976	169,150	173,246	176,052
	Principals	132	132	132	133	141	148
	Per-pupil expenditures, in dollars	9,531	9,359	9,216	9,687	9,697	

Table 2.3—Continued

District	Driver	2010–2011	2011–2012	2012–2013	2013–2014	2014–2015	2015–2016
New York City	Pupils		1,089,537	1,094,945	1,104,479	1,122,783	1,133,963
	Principals		1,654	1,706	1,781	1,821	1,856
	Per-pupil expenditures, in dollars	16,178	16,525	16,610	17,311	17,297	
Prince George's	Pupils	127,039	126,671	123,833	123,737	125,136	127,576
	Principals	210	213	212	211	213	216
	Per-pupil expenditures, in dollars	11,413	11,260	11,800	11,701	11,720	

NOTE: In cases for which data for 2010–2011 were unavailable, we used data for 2011–2012. In the cases for which data for 2011–2012 were unavailable, we used data from the prior year. For per-pupil expenditures, in particular, data were not publicly available beyond 2013–2014 in some cases. In those cases, we adjusted 2013–2014 per-pupil expenditures by 2014–2015 RPPs, and we used the 2014–2015 data for 2015–2016 (because RPPs beyond 2014–2015 were not available). In addition, we used 2014–2015 data for the numbers of pupils and principals in Hillsborough because pupil and principal numbers were not available through the Florida Department of Education.

to readers: (1) a comprehensive list of potential activities with their costs that could be part of district efforts to build and improve their principal pipelines and (2) guidance regarding the potential district costs for these efforts overall and for specific pipeline activities. We used an activity-based approach to develop our list of potential principal pipeline activities and gather data from individual districts. We made decisions about what to include in and exclude from our cost estimates. Each decision has associated challenges and limitations. Nevertheless, our work provides a unique look at the cost of building and maintaining principal pipelines in urban school districts. We know of no other studies that provide this level of cost information and provide resources that can help any district reflect on how it might work to build a principal pipeline based on what is possible in its own context. This report also points to gaps in spending for some districts compared with others and might inform additional work to understand payoff of investments in terms of improved principal and school outcomes.

CHAPTER THREE

Findings on Pipeline Costs Overall and by Major Category

In this first findings chapter of our report, we present estimates of overall principal pipeline costs and costs for each major category of pipeline activity, as well as trends in principal pipeline spending, by category, from year to year. We organize these findings by major pipeline category so that we can explore all the costs for each component and describe different ways of considering those costs. In Chapter Four, we consider investment and staffing expenditures for principal pipelines. As noted in Chapter Two, describing our approach, we adjusted all resources and expenditures included in our findings for regional purchasing power and inflation.

Overall Principal Pipeline Resources and Expenditures

Table 3.1 provides the average annual resources and expenditures across all districts participating in the Principal Pipeline Initiative, including the overall average annual costs and the costs when taking into account particular cost drivers for each district; the number of principals or pupils in each district; and the costs, as a percentage, of per-pupil expenditures in each district. Our estimate of average annual resources and expenditures for the initiative takes into account the first four SYs of the initiative, from 2011–2012 to 2014–2015. We do not include costs for 2015–2016 in our average annual cost estimates, given that these estimates are extrapolations. However, we do refer to data about average resources and expenditures for 2015–2016 when we examine change in costs, by year, for each major category.

The maximum and minimum costs in Table 3.1 represent the costs for the district that spent the most and least on each category. The district with the maximum costs for a particular category might not be the same district with the maximum per-principal or per-pupil costs, and, similarly, the district with the minimum costs for a particular category might not be the same district with the minimum per-principal or per-pupil costs. Figure 3.1 provides the same data as Table 3.1 but on a per-principal basis only. Throughout this report, we generally focus on per-principal costs for consistency's sake, although we occasionally present data by other cost drivers in special cases. Figure 3.2 presents the percentage of total pipeline costs devoted to each major

Table 3.1
Average Annual Resources and Expenditures for Principal Pipeline Initiative Districts for School Years 2011–2012 Through 2014–2015, by Cost Driver

	All Costs, in Dollars			Per-Principal Costs, in Dollars			Per-Pupil Costs, in Dollars			Percentage of All District Expenditures		
Category	Average	Minimum	Maximum	Average	Minimum	Maximum	Average	Minimum	Maximum	Average	Minimum	Maximum
Leader standards	90,299	28,080	262,851	292	179	547	0.41	0.17	0.95	0.004	0.001	0.010
Preservice preparation	2,892,639	783,714	9,226,567	9,386	2,907	23,015	13.27	3.80	39.49	0.123	0.044	0.397
Selective hiring and placement	475,605	220,516	785,723	2,894	817	5,867	3.57	1.07	5.17	0.036	0.012	0.049
On-the-job support and evaluation	2,718,385	1,614,059	5,309,588	13,956	10,903	19,790	18.53	9.86	25.91	0.193	0.103	0.303
Systems and capacity for supporting the initiative	672,252	260,575	1,148,870	3,425	176	5,406	4.69	0.30	9.16	0.047	0.002	0.079

NOTE: We adjusted costs for regional purchasing power and inflation. We excluded New York City from cost estimates for selective hiring and placement and on-the-job support and evaluation. Preservice costs were highest of any category in terms of overall costs, but on-the-job support and evaluation had a higher cost after application of cost drivers because of variation in costs across larger and smaller districts.

Figure 3.1
Average Annual Per-Principal Resources and Expenditures, by Major Category, School Years 2011–2012 Through 2014–2015

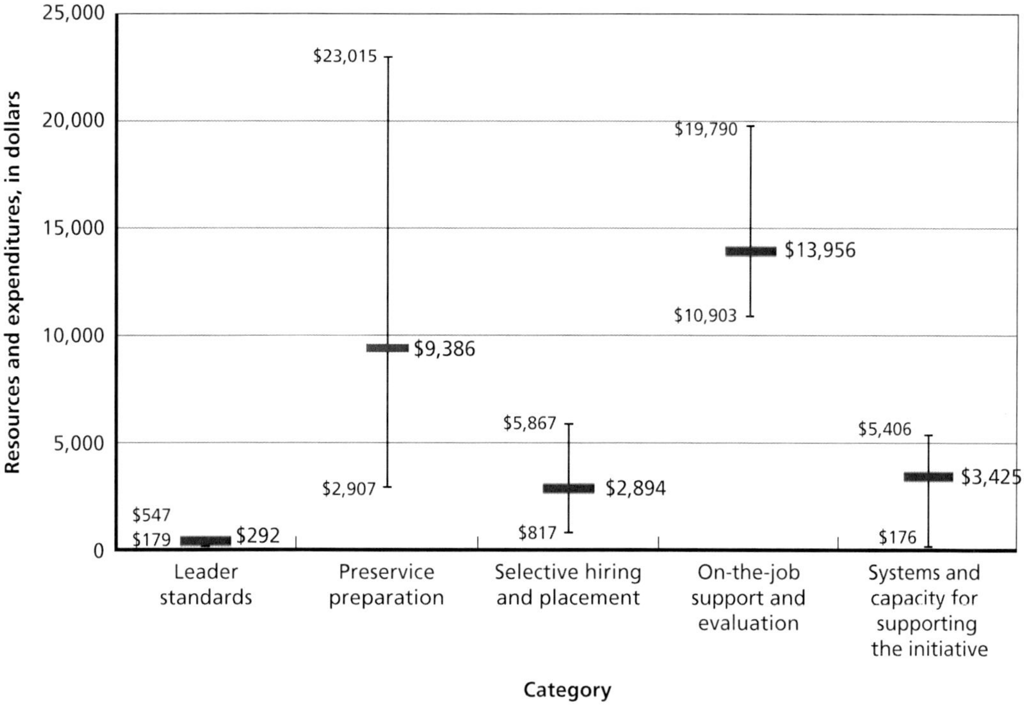

NOTE: The purple bar for each component represents the average of the overall costs in each district. Because we have cost estimates for spending on only three of the five major pipeline categories for New York City, we did not include data for that city for the two missing categories (selective hiring and placement and on-the-job support and evaluation). The error bar for each year shows the range from the district with the highest resources and expenditures to the one with the lowest resources and expenditures for each component.

RAND *RR2078-3.1*

category. Each estimate of overall average pipeline costs represents an average of the overall costs in each district. We do not include data from New York City in overall average annual resource and expenditure estimates because we have cost estimates for spending on only three of the five major pipeline categories in New York City.

For all major categories of pipeline activities, districts spent about $5.6 million each year, on average, which translates to a little more than $31,000 per principal or $42 per pupil per year. For all districts, this is just a small fraction of their total per-pupil expenditures in each year. As can be seen in the table and figures, districts spent much more on the preservice preparation and on-the-job support and evaluation categories of the principal pipeline (approximately $9,400 and $14,000 per principal, respectively) than on other categories. Together, preservice preparation and on-the-job support and evaluation for principals and APs accounted for about three-quarters of all

Figure 3.2
Percentage of Total Principal Pipeline Resources and Expenditures Devoted to Each Major Category, School Years 2011–2012 Through 2014–2015

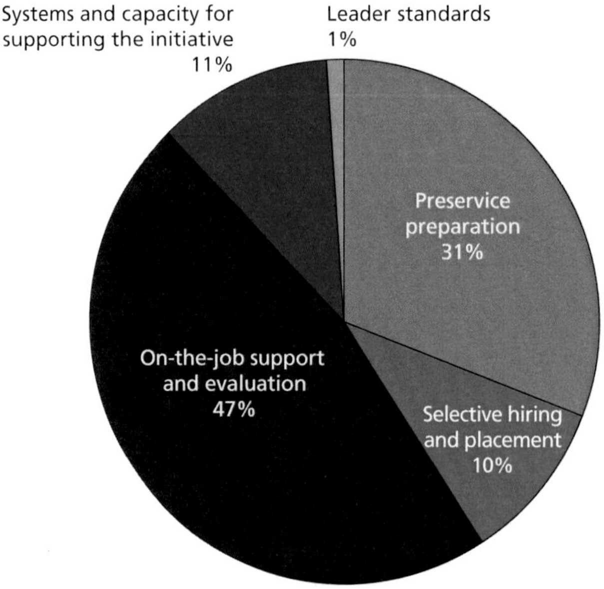

NOTES: We based the percentages on our estimates of total principal pipeline resources and expenditures for school years 2011–2012 through 2014–2015 for the five Principal Pipeline Initiative districts for which we had data for all categories of pipeline activities (i.e., excludes New York City).

RAND *RR2078-3.2*

principal pipeline expenditures. Furthermore, the range of costs for preservice and on-the-job support and evaluation activities—particularly the range of preservice preparation costs—was much larger than the ranges for the other categories. The higher cost and large range for preservice preparation resources and expenditures reflect districts' different approaches to preservice preparation. In contrast, the cost of the leader standards category was particularly small, at only $292 per principal or $90,299 annually; leader standards resources and expenditures took up just 1 percent of all pipeline costs.

Figure 3.3 illustrates the change in overall principal pipeline costs over time. Spending on principal pipeline activities changed considerably over time across participating districts. For the year prior to the start of the initiative, we estimate that average district spending on principal pipeline activities was a little less than $9,400 per principal. Our estimate for the preinitiative period might exclude relevant costs that districts did not track. For the first SY of the initiative (2011–2012), we estimate principal pipeline costs to be more than twice that amount, at $20,264 per principal. From 2011–2012 to 2014–2015, average resources and expenditures steadily grew to nearly

Figure 3.3
Average Per-Principal Resources and Expenditures, by Year, for All Principal Pipeline Activities

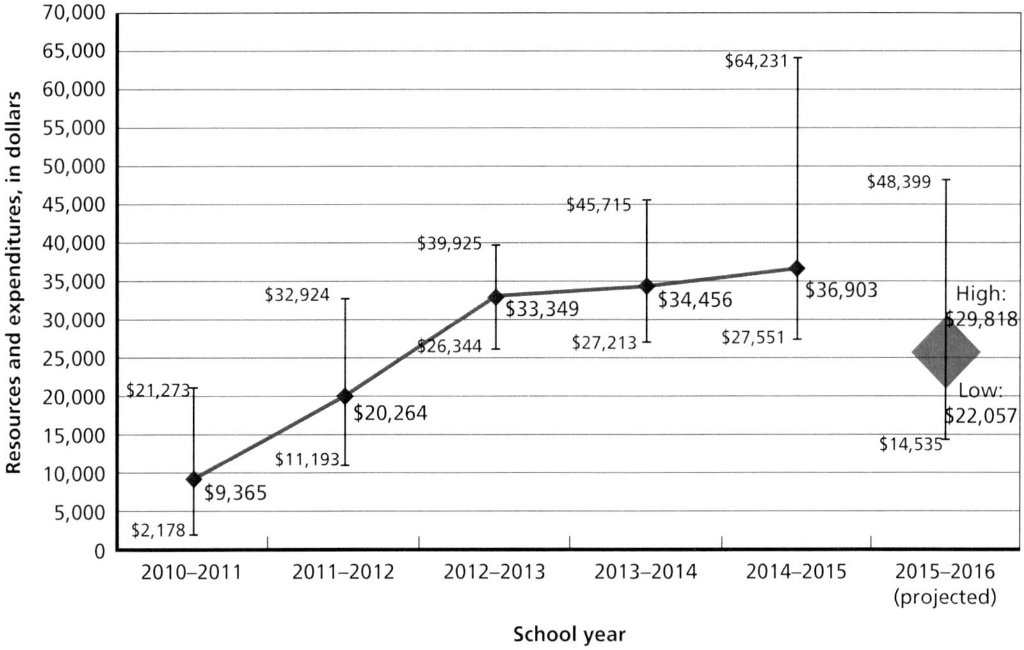

NOTE: The purple diamonds represent the estimates of average principal pipeline expenditures across the five Principal Pipeline Initiative districts for which we have data for all categories of pipeline activities (i.e., excludes New York City). The lower bound or minimum average cost (as depicted by the bottom of the diamond for 2015–2016) represents projected costs when only personnel costs are doubled. The upper bound or maximum average cost (as depicted by the top of the diamond for 2015–2016) represents projected costs when all costs—personnel and nonpersonnel—are doubled. The error bar for each year shows the range from the district with the highest resources and expenditures to the one with the lowest resources and expenditures.

RAND *RR2078-3.3*

$37,000 per principal and then declined somewhat in 2015–2016; the predicted range of principal pipeline costs for 2015–2016 was between about $22,000 and $29,800.

Readers should keep in mind that—as we noted in Chapter Two—the estimates of 2015–2016 costs are extrapolations based on data from the first half of 2015–2016. The lower bound or minimum average cost (as depicted by the bottom of the diamond in Figure 3.3 for 2015–2016) represents projected costs when only personnel costs are doubled. The upper bound or maximum average cost (as depicted by the top of the diamond for 2015–2016) represents projected costs when all costs—personnel and nonpersonnel—are doubled. The error bar in the figure for each year shows the range from the district with the highest resources and expenditures to the one with the lowest resources and expenditures for leader standards. For 2015–2016, the minimum costs are for the district with the lowest projected resources and expenditures when only personnel costs are doubled, whereas the maximum resources and expenditures are for the district with the highest projected costs when all costs are doubled.

Readers might be struck by the steady rise in average pipeline costs from 2011–2012 to 2014–2015 in Figure 3.3. However, it is important to keep in mind that these annual costs represent averages across six districts, and districts with particularly large increases in costs can pull that average up. After 2012–2013, pipeline costs increased in only two of the five participating districts—excluding New York City because we lacked costs for two categories of pipeline activities there—and costs decreased in the other districts. One district in particular experienced a rise in costs of nearly $25,000 per principal from 2012–2013 to 2014–2015, mostly because of rises in preservice costs. If we remove that district from our cost estimates, overall costs decrease by about $1,800 from 2012–2013 to 2014–2015. In addition, increases in costs for some of the later years of the initiative could reflect the approaching end of grant funding for the initiative. For example, districts might be expected to spend more toward the end of their grant funding than they might spend if funding were not expected to end. Nonetheless, the slight decrease in spending for the last six months of the initiative suggests that districts could have also adjusted their spending patterns to be more conservative, given the anticipated end of Wallace funding.

Resources and Expenditures Devoted to Component 1: Leader Standards

State school leader standards—when present—and Professional Standards for Educational Leaders developed and updated by the National Policy Board for Educational Administration served as essential guides for leader standard development. However, as noted by Turnbull, Anderson, et al., 2016, each district developed and used leader standards as a powerful tool to "align [district] actions and policies to their priorities for school leadership" (p. 9). Leader standards provided key guidance for the design and development of preservice preparation programs, hiring foci, and ways to support and evaluate principals. Turnbull, Anderson, et al., 2016, states that leader standard development "was not a one-time event" (p. iii). Instead, districts regularly revisited their standards in order to reflect on leader standard foci and what those foci mean for other pieces of the pipeline. Turnbull, Anderson, et al., 2016, also notes that changes to other pipeline activities—such as hiring and principal evaluation—sometimes spurred districts to revisit and revise their standards. Box 3.1 summarizes the main takeaways from our analysis of pipeline expenditure information related to leader standards.

If leader standards were indeed a powerful tool for supporting the principal pipeline, as our analysis of the data suggested, work on leader standards was also remarkably inexpensive compared with other principal pipeline categories. As noted in Table 3.1,

Box 3.1

Key Takeaways: Resources Devoted to Leader Standards

- Districts devoted fewer resources to the development and refinement of leader standards than to other principal pipeline categories.
- Leader standards work was not a one-time proposition; districts devoted resources to leader standards in each year of the initiative.
- Some districts front-loaded their leader standards work early in the initiative, whereas other emphasized this work toward the end of the initiative.
- More than 80 percent of the costs of leader standards efforts were costs for personnel time to develop and refine the standards.
- Total district costs for leader standards activities appear to be influenced by the districts' starting point on leader standards rather than by district size.

the cost of leader standards was, on average, just $292 per principal annually, or a total annual average cost of $90,299. The range of costs for leader standards across the participating districts was also relatively small, with minimum annual average costs of $28,080 (or $179 per principal) in one district and maximum annual average costs of $262,851 (or $547 per principal) in another district.

Expenditures on leader standards do not appear to be driven by district size, as measured by the number of students or the number of principals. The three lower-spending districts each spent between $180,000 and $220,000 on leader standards efforts over the time frame of the initiative. The three districts that spent the most on leader standards were quite different from one another in terms of the cost drivers that we considered for our study. Overall, spending on leader standards efforts seemed to be influenced by whether the district already had leader standards (from the district or the state) at the start of the initiative and the breadth of engagement in the leader standards effort within the district.

Our analysis reinforces that the development of leader standards was not a one-time event. As seen in Figure 3.4, the average costs of leader standards across all districts ramped up from 2010–2011 to 2011–2012, as districts began to invest more time and effort on leader standards. However, many districts reported doing at least some work to think about their leader standards prior to 2011–2012, which is why we note some leader standards costs in 2010–2011. Costs for leader standards then steadily decreased from after 2011–2012 to 2014–2015. However, the projected average costs of leader standards in 2015–2016 were even higher than the average costs in 2011–2012. The observed average resources and expenditures for the first half of 2015–2016 were about the same as those for the entire 2014–2015 SY, and the high and low range of projected costs for 2015–2016 was also higher than spending in 2014–2015. These data thus suggest that resources and expenditures devoted to leader standards were higher in 2015–2016 than in 2014–2015.

Figure 3.4
Average Per-Principal Resources and Expenditures, by Year, for Leader Standards Activities

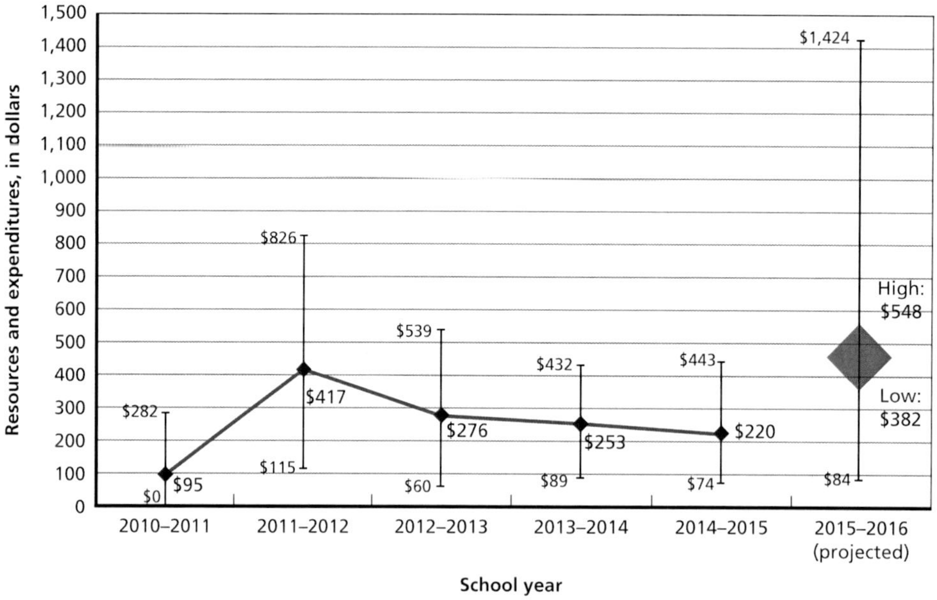

NOTE: The purple diamonds represent the estimates of average principal pipeline expenditures across all Principal Pipeline Initiative districts. The lower bound or minimum average cost (as depicted by the bottom of the diamond for 2015–2016) represents projected costs when only personnel costs are doubled. The upper bound or maximum average cost (as depicted by the top of the diamond for 2015–2016) represents projected costs when all costs—personnel and nonpersonnel—are doubled. The error bar for each year shows the range from the district with the highest resources and expenditures to the one with the lowest resources and expenditures.

RAND *RR2078-3.4*

This increase for 2015–2016 was due to a rise in leader standard development costs in two districts that utilized Wallace funding to pay consultants who supported further reflection and work on leader standards. The National Policy Board for Educational Administration released the Professional Standards for Educational Leaders in October 2015, the first update to the Interstate School Leaders Licensure Consortium Standards since 2008. This major revision to national standards might have prompted a focus on leader standards at the district level and a rise in costs for leader standard revision activities in 2015–2016.

More than 80 percent of the annual average costs for leader standards were costs for personnel. Specifically, the annual average costs of district personnel who contributed their time to examination of leader standards were $244 per principal (compared with the annual average costs of $292 for all leader standards work). In most districts, the key district personnel who contributed substantial portions of their time to work on other pipeline categories—such as preservice preparation for school leaders or on-the-job support for principals—also invested time on the development and refinement of leader standards. As noted in Turnbull, Anderson, et al., 2016, many districts formed committees composed of district administration and other personnel—including principals themselves, in some districts[1]—who met regularly to discuss and refine leader standards. Thus, although the costs of leader standards were low, our analysis indicates that they did take some district personnel time in every year. Districts need to consider the opportunity cost of this time, which could have been directed to other important activities related or unrelated to principal pipelines. The costs for leader standards beyond personnel costs were mostly costs for consultants who helped districts reflect on and improve their leader standards.

Even though annual average costs for leader standards decreased from 2011–2012 to 2014–2015, that decrease masks some shifts in annual average costs for leader standards in each year. The projected costs for leader standards in 2015–2016 were higher than costs in previous years for two participating districts. However, in one district, leader standards costs were highest in SY 2012–2013 because that was the year during which they had the most personnel and time invested in that work. In three other districts, costs for leader standards were highest in 2011–2012, at the start of the initiative. However, our analysis suggests that costs of leader standards will likely fluctuate across districts for the foreseeable future as districts revisit their leader standards and continually use them to guide and shape their pipelines.

Resources and Expenditures Devoted to Component 2: Preservice Preparation

District spending for preservice preparation includes resources devoted to operating preservice programs for both principals and APs, revising preservice preparation for principals and APs, and overseeing the quality of the portfolio of programs. Preservice preparation program operation encompasses candidate recruitment, screening and selection for preservice programs, and the delivery of preservice programs.

From the start of the initiative, leaders in participating districts took varied approaches to strengthen the district role in the preparation of principals and to align program features with research-based recommendations for high-quality preservice preparation (see Turnbull, Anderson, et al., 2016, p. 15). At the start of the initiative, participating districts differed substantially in terms of their overall involvement in preservice preparation and in the extent to which they relied on in-house programs versus external partners for preservice preparation. A primary concern of most of the participating districts at the launch of the initiative was developing a pool of high-quality candidates for leadership positions (Turnbull, Riley, Arcaira, et al., 2013). By the end of the initiative, many districts characterized their candidate pools as robust

---

[1] As noted above, we excluded the cost of time spent by principals and APs from our estimates unless they received a payment or stipend for their work.

and were discussing challenges related to keeping good candidates motivated while awaiting a vacancy (Turnbull, Anderson, et al., 2016). During the initiative, participating districts developed new in-house programs and external partnerships and worked to improve existing ones through the Quality Measures process and other efforts. Despite the variation in strategies that participating districts pursued for preservice preparation, two common emphases emerged. First, all participating districts took a more active role in identifying preservice candidates over the course of the initiative, using data collected through LTSs. And, second, all participating districts worked to improve clinical learning experiences for preservice candidates.

The initiative was grounded in research that emphasized the importance of on-the-job or clinical learning experiences (Darling-Hammond et al., 2007). Participating districts undertook efforts to enhance these clinical experiences in both in-house and external programs, experimenting with a variety of approaches for identifying clinical sites and mentors and structuring the experiences. Clinical experiences can be provided in the context of an aspiring leader's current position or through placement in a new setting under the guidance of a high-quality leader or mentor principal. The second option—placement in a new setting—is usually referred to as a residency for a school leader candidate. The duration of the residency for specific preservice programs in participating districts varied from a month to an entire SY (Turnbull, Anderson, et al., 2016, p. 19). During the initiative, three of the districts dramatically expanded the clinical aspect of their programs (Turnbull, Anderson, et al., 2016, p. 19). Other districts supported clinical experiences for preservice programs from external providers.

Although preservice preparation was a focus for all participating districts during the initiative, assessing the effect of any changes in the quality of new principals will take time. Turnbull, Anderson, et al., 2016, indicates that the time between the start of principal preservice and placement as a principal in a participating district ranged from three to ten years.

Box 3.2 summarizes the main takeaways from our analysis of pipeline resource and expenditure information related to preservice preparation activities.

The adjusted average annual cost of preservice preparation was about $2.9 million per year (see Table 3.1), which translates to about $9,400 per principal or $13 per pupil. Spending on preservice preparation was also extremely variable across districts, which is unsurprising given the array of approaches and programs in the participating districts. As reflected in Table 3.1 and Figure 3.1, the annual average resources and expenditures for preservice preparation in the district that spent the least on those activities were about $2,900 per principal, whereas the annual average resources and expenditures in the district that spent the most on preservice preparation were about $23,000 per principal. Also as seen in Table 3.1, adjusted average annual costs for preservice preparation were higher than for all other pipeline categories. However, when measured on a per-principal or per-pupil basis, on-the-job support and evaluation had a higher cost. Readers should keep in mind that per-principal estimates are based on

Box 3.2

Key Takeaways: Resources Devoted to Preservice Preparation

- The work to plan for and maintain preservice preparation programs was relatively small compared with the cost of actually running preservice preparation on an ongoing basis.
- A little more than three-quarters of all costs for the preservice preparation component were devoted to the delivery of preservice preparation.
- Districts adopted vastly different approaches to supporting preservice preparation, and this is reflected in wide variation in expenditures across districts.
- Stipends provided to those participating in principal residencies that were a part of some preservice preparation programs represented a large portion of the costs for those programs.

the total number of principals currently serving in each district, not on the number of people who have completed preservice programs in a given year. The people going through a preservice program in a given year are not serving as principals—rather, they are potential candidates for future principal vacancies. Per-principal and per-pupil costs are intended to provide readers with cost estimates that account for district and school size. In some additional analysis below, we also examine costs per preservice program completer.

Figure 3.5 illustrates the resources and expenditures by preservice preparation activity. As seen here, a little more than three-quarters of all costs for preservice preparation were for preservice preparation program delivery. Preservice preparation delivery costs were about $7,250 per principal annually, on average. Preservice preparation delivery could include any personnel focused on delivering preservice preparation programming (mostly the case for internal, district-led programs); costs (including tuition) for any external subcontractors the district paid to prepare principals or APs; spending for materials, supplies, facility rental, tuition reimbursement, or any other nonpersonnel costs that districts bore; and payments to program participants for residencies that were part of some preservice programs.

Beyond preservice preparation delivery, other preservice preparation activities that had costs included districts' work to revise the preservice preparation system, recruit candidates for preservice preparation, screen and select candidates for preservice preparation, and oversee the whole district portfolio of preservice preparation programs. But costs for all these activities apart from preservice preparation delivery were only 23 percent of the total preservice preparation cost and did not vary a great deal from district to district. Thus, we surmise that the resources and expenditures necessary to plan for and maintain preservice preparation programs are relatively small and stable compared with the cost of operating preservice preparation programs on an ongoing basis.

Figure 3.5
Average Annual Per-Principal Resources and Expenditures for Preservice Activities, School Years 2011–2012 Through 2014–2015

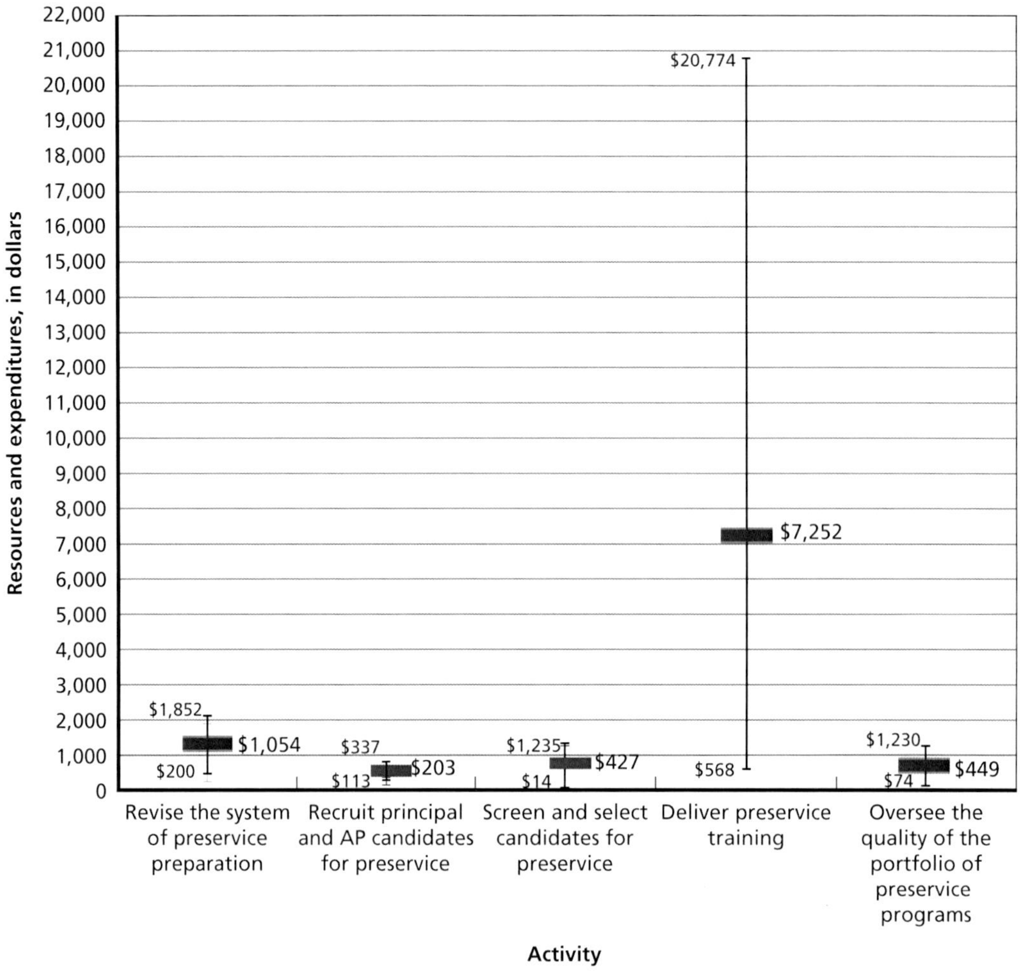

NOTE: The purple bar for each component represents the average of the overall costs in each district. The error bar for each year shows the range from the district with the highest resources and expenditures to the one with the lowest resources and expenditures.
RAND *RR2078-3.5*

It is worth noting that aspiring leaders who received administrative licensure rarely moved directly from such programs into principalships. Among first- and second-year principals whom PSA surveyed in the spring of 2015, "the median elapsed time from starting preparation to becoming a principal had been six years" (Turnbull, Anderson, et al., 2016, p. 20). More typically, these aspiring leaders first become APs and were then appointed to principalships after gaining experience as APs. We categorized resources devoted to programs intended to provide licensure or preparation for aspiring leaders who had not yet become APs as AP preservice preparation expenditures, whereas we categorized resources for programs intended to provide preparation for the principalship, often (but not always) offered to current APs, as principal preservice preparation expenditures.

Turnbull, Anderson, et al., 2016, describes the trade-offs that districts face in designing robust clinical experiences for principal preparation, noting that "moving aspiring principals out of their schools for a residency in a different school could be disruptive and expensive" (p. 22). Our analysis confirms this sentiment that districts reported. We found that residencies made up a large portion of the costs for delivery of preservice preparation programs. Three districts had principal and AP residencies as part of their preservice preparation programs. Payments to principals to do these residencies or payments to the substitutes hired to fill in for them while on residency—as well as smaller payments to mentors overseeing the residencies—represented a large portion of preservice preparation costs in those districts. In districts where preservice preparation programs did not involve payments for residencies, preservice preparation expenditures were much lower. Given that residency costs were sometimes intertwined with other preservice costs within districts, we cannot provide precise dollar amounts for the cost of residencies. That said, average annual per-principal costs for preservice preparation in districts that did not have residency programs were $5,168, whereas they were $13,604 in districts with residency programs.

The costs for residencies contributed to the generally higher costs for delivery on a per-principal basis of internal preservice programs within districts compared with costs for delivery of preservice programs through partnerships that districts had with external preservice providers. Specifically, the delivery of internal preservice preparation programs for principals or APs costs districts an annual average of $5,640 per principal or an annual average cost of nearly $1.5 million, whereas the delivery associated with external partnerships for principals or APs—typically spent through district subcontracts with preservice providers—costs districts an annual average of $1,612 per principal or an annual average cost of a little less than $656,000. Furthermore, the range of costs for internal programs was very large: from a minimum of just $108 in one district that had one small internal program to prepare APs to a maximum of $19,928 in another district that operated several internal programs to prepare APs and principals. In contrast, the range for costs of partnerships with external preparation programs was much smaller: from $0 in one district that did not focus on preservice program delivery for external partnerships to $4,747 in another district with several preservice partnerships for preparation of both APs and principals. Some but not all of the external partners offered residency-based programs. That said, as we noted in Chapter One, our cost analysis does not take into account all the potential costs borne by external providers. Staff at some institutions who provided preservice in partnership with districts might have contributed a great deal of time and effort to preservice partnerships for which we do not account in district expenditures to subcontracts or consultants. Additionally, some external partners relied on tuition payments from participants, and those are not accounted for here.

Personnel costs for preservice preparation were relatively low compared with personnel costs for other pipeline categories. Just over one-quarter of all annual average resources and expenditures for preservice preparation were for district personnel. Unsurprisingly, most of the district personnel costs for preservice preparation delivery were in internal, district-led programs. Specifically, a little less than one-third of the costs for district-led principal and AP programs were for personnel. In contrast, districts reported no personnel costs for delivery of external preservice preparation programs for principals, and personnel costs made up less than 1 percent of the costs for delivery of external AP preservice preparation programs. This does not mean that district personnel did not spend any time supporting these external programs. Instead, that personnel time is likely documented under other preservice preparation activities, such as work on the revision and development of programs overall and overseeing the quality of districts' preservice preparation portfolios.

The trends in district spending for preservice preparation are also interesting to consider. Figure 3.6 suggests that the costs for preservice preparation actually increased in districts over time to a high of almost $12,000 per principal in 2014–2015, although variability in district spending also increased from 2011–2012 to 2014–2015. These year-to-year changes in costs for preservice preparation—and variability in preservice preparation costs—stem mainly from change and variability in one particular preservice preparation activity: delivery of preservice preparation. Costs for delivery of preservice preparation increased from an average annual cost of almost $3,400 in 2011–2012 to about $10,000 in 2014–2015.

The largest rise in preservice costs occurred from 2011–2012 to 2012–2013. In this year, the costs of preservice rose in all but one district, with costs for the specific activity of preservice delivery rising the most. The rise in costs from 2012–2013 to 2013–2014 and 2013–2014 to 2014–2015 stemmed from rises in preservice costs—and particularly preservice delivery costs—in three districts. One district experienced particularly high rises in preservice delivery costs in all these years, mostly as the result of that district's investments in preservice preparation for APs, including stipends for differentiated teacher leader roles as a way to encourage a career ladder from teaching to the principalship. As we point out below, these rises in costs for preservice delivery somewhat follow increases in the numbers of candidates completing preservice programs, although the number of completers does not completely explain increased preservice delivery costs.

We also examined the extent to which increases in preservice preparation program delivery costs in particular reflected growth in the numbers of people participating in and graduating from preservice preparation programs. Districts provided information on the numbers of people who completed the preferred preservice preparation programs on which they focused their resources and expenditures each year.

Figure 3.6
Average Per-Principal Resources and Expenditures, by Year, for Preservice Activities

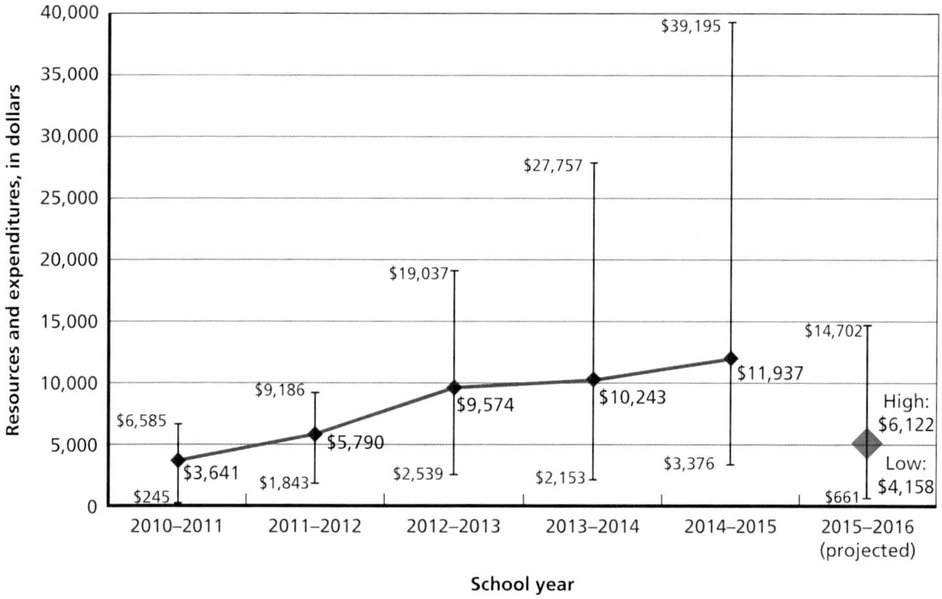

NOTE: The purple diamonds represent the estimates of average principal pipeline expenditures across all Principal Pipeline Initiative districts. The lower bound or minimum average cost (as depicted by the bottom of the diamond for 2015–2016) represents projected costs when only personnel costs are doubled. The upper bound or maximum average cost (as depicted by the top of the diamond for 2015–2016) represents projected costs when all costs—personnel and nonpersonnel—are doubled. The error bar for each year shows the range from the district with the highest resources and expenditures to the one with the lowest resources and expenditures.

RAND *RR2078-3.6*

In Table 3.2, we present the average number of people completing preservice preparation programs in each year, from 2011–2012 through 2014–2015, along with the average cost of preservice preparation delivery (just that one activity within the preservice preparation component) by principal preparation program completer. Readers should not interpret these costs as costs of "tuition" for a program completer. Instead, these costs encompass everything that goes into the actual delivery of preservice, from costs of instructors and training materials to any technology used for instructional delivery to district payments for residents and those who support residents.

As seen in Table 3.2, the average number of participants completing preservice preparation programs did increase over time, from an average of just 53 completers in 2012 to an average of 170 in 2015. The largest jumps in program completions occurred between 2011–2012 and 2012–2013 and between 2012–2013 and 2013–2014. These rises in preservice completions can be partially attributed to a growing focus on preparation programs for APs in some districts, but they also reflect an effort on the part of some districts to build the pool of principal candidates during the time frame of the initiative. No districts documented having any preferred providers for AP preparation

Table 3.2
Average Number of People Completing Principal Preservice Programs and Resources and Expenditures per Program Participant for Preservice Delivery in Each Year

SY	Average Number of Completions	Cost per Completer, in Dollars		
		Average	Minimum	Maximum
2011–2012	53	36,967	477	76,684
2012–2013	121	28,726	1,007	71,244
2013–2014	166	30,879	1,633	75,826
2014–2015	170	27,296	951	67,417
Average	128	30,967	1,017	58,962

NOTE: The minimum costs each year result in the average because the same district is represented in each year. This is not the case for the maximum costs, so the average is not the average of the numbers in that column.

in 2011–2012. Thus, we did not document any AP program completers in that year. However, by 2014–2015, five districts had developed external partnerships or created internal programs intended to prepare people specifically for AP positions.

As can also be seen in the table, the average cost per completer was highest at the start of the initiative, in 2011–2012 (at nearly $37,000 per completer), and then decreased to a low of $27,296 per program completer in 2014–2015. As noted previously, although the rise in the numbers of those completing preservice programs tracks somewhat with rises in total preservice delivery costs (as noted in Figure 3.6), the number of completers does not fully explain changes in preservice costs or cost per completer over time. We surmise that the change in costs might also be connected to district decisions regarding how much school leader preparation they are willing to subsidize. In some cases, particularly when districts partnered with external programs, program participants might have paid more of the costs themselves. We caution readers against interpreting these figures as a cost for particular principal preservice preparation programs. As mentioned previously, many districts were devoting resources to preservice preparation for APs as well as principals, especially during later years of the initiative.

Another observation from Table 3.2 is that there is wide variation in annual spending per program completer. This wide variation reflects the large differences among preservice preparation programs and their costs. In four districts, for example, average annual spending per preservice preparation program completer was more than $50,000 in at least one year, whereas the costs in the two other districts were under $5,000 per preservice preparation program completer in some years. Box 3.3 summarizes information about additional expenditures for preservice preparation that aspiring leaders bore themselves, which we do not directly include in our estimates.

As with leader standards, we found that expenditures for preservice preparation were not always clearly related to our measures of district size. Although districts with more principals typically have more principal vacancies to fill in a given year, even the number of school leader vacancies in school districts did not directly drive the number of preservice candidates supported by the district or total spending on preservice. Other factors, such as the quality of the candidate pool at the start of the initiative, growth in the number of schools in the district, and strategic decisions about how to support preservice, likely also play a significant role in preservice costs. At the same time, as we mentioned in Chapter One, most of the participating districts are relatively similar in terms of numbers of pupils and schools. Thus, we have limited ability to pinpoint ways in which district size drives costs.

Two strategic district decisions that could affect preservice costs borne by the district are worth noting. The first is a decision regarding the share of preservice preparation costs borne by the district versus the aspiring leader. Some participating districts chose to cover some or all of the cost of preservice preparation for some or most candidates. This approach provided the district with an opportunity to influence who pursued preservice preparation, as well as the content of the preservice preparation. How-

Box 3.3

Preservice Preparation Costs from Novice Principals' and Assistant Principals' Perspectives

Although our study focused on costs from the district perspective, it is important for districts to acknowledge that people incur out-of-pocket financial costs associated with preparation. The survey that PSA administered to novice principals and APs asked administrators about their total out-of-pocket expenditures for tuition and other expenditures related to administrative licensure and AP or principal preparation programs that the district did not reimburse. Novice principals surveyed in 2014–2015 reported spending an average of $3,747 on their preservice preparation, and novice APs surveyed in 2014–2015 reported spending an average of $4,931 on their preservice preparation.

Overall, the average spending by individuals on preservice preparation—as noted through their principal and AP survey responses—was not as variable across districts as the districts' spending on preservice preparation activities. Across districts, novice principals reported spending an average of $2,119 to $4,966, and novice APs reported spending an average of $2,701 to $9,264. Interestingly, novice principals' and APs' average spending on preservice preparation tended to be lower in districts spending higher average amounts on preservice preparation. This suggests that some districts might be paying a greater share of preservice preparation costs than their trainees. Yet, spending on preservice preparation at the individual level was extremely variable within districts, which likely corresponds to differences in preservice preparation programs.

ever, districts face a risk that program completers might not become principals in the district after completion. Districts balance the costs of investing in preservice preparation with other considerations, such as the district culture and local labor market conditions. The most sensible approach for one district might not work for another district. The other strategic district choice that would affect the cost of preservice is the choice between spending on preservice preparation and spending on induction and on-the-job support. The participating district that spends the least on preservice preparation might end up spending the most on on-the-job support. One leader in a participating district described this as a "pay now or pay later" perspective.

Resources and Expenditures Devoted to Component 3: Selective Hiring and Placement

Resources devoted to selective hiring and placement include the resources involved in recruiting, screening, and hiring school leaders, as well as resources devoted to revising hiring and placement systems. Top district leaders viewed the changes made to hiring and placement during the initiative as successful (Turnbull, Anderson, et al., 2016, p. 25). In addition, a higher fraction of principals who started on the job between 2013 and 2015 felt that their skills were an excellent fit with the needs of their schools than novice principals who started from 2010 to 2012 did (Turnbull, Anderson, et al., 2016, p. 33). All participating districts undertook efforts to make hiring and placement processes more systematic, rooted in leader standards and guided by objective data. Two of the districts had already taken steps in that direction at the time the initiative was launched, and the others quickly followed their lead. All districts worked over the course of the initiative to refine these processes by engaging in vacancy planning, creating hiring pools or selection stages, and using simulation exercises to assess candidates' skills against their leader standards. Districts also developed and used data systems to inform hiring and placement processes (Turnbull, Anderson, et al., 2016, pp. 25–36). It is too early to conclusively assess the implications that the hiring investments or investments in other categories of the pipeline had for turnover in participating districts. However, our preliminary analysis of available data from participating districts suggests that, in three of the districts, the percentage of newly hired principals who continue to serve as principals in the district after two years increased substantially between 2010–2011 and 2013–2014.

Box 3.4 summarizes the main takeaways from our analysis of pipeline cost information related to selective hiring and placement. As with leader standards and preservice, we found that expenditures for selective hiring and placement were not strongly related to district size.

Figure 3.7 describes the average spending on selective hiring and placement activities during the time frame of the initiative. On average, across districts and across

Box 3.4

Key Takeaways: Resources Devoted to Selective Hiring and Placement

- On average, districts devoted a small share of total pipeline resources to selective hiring and placement (about 9 percent of all pipeline expenditures), amounting to $2,894 per principal or $3.57 per pupil.
- Nearly half of the resources devoted to hiring and placement during the initiative were investments in revisions to hiring systems.
- Compared with ranges for other pipeline categories, the range of expenditures across districts was narrow; much of the variation stemmed from differences in resources devoted to system improvements.

years, participating districts devoted $2,894 per principal or $3.57 per pupil each year to selective hiring activities. The range of costs was $817 per principal to $5,867 per principal—much narrower than for preservice preparation.

Forty-six percent of that spending ($1,338 per principal) was devoted to revising the system of principal screening, hiring, and placement. However, the high average costs for revision of hiring and placement were particularly driven by high costs in one district that spent more than $4,000 per principal each year, on average, on hiring and placement revision activities. In that district, hiring and placement revision activities included the time and effort of some district personnel who weighed in on revisions, subcontracts with organizations and people who helped the district evaluate and revise its recruitment and hiring efforts, and work to design the tools used to evaluate candidates and train personnel to administer those tools. If that district were excluded from our analysis, the cost of hiring and placement revision activities would be about $650 per principal.

Variation in resources devoted to recruiting, candidate pool screening and interviewing, and hiring school leaders reflected differences in local contexts, as well as differences in the way principal pipelines operated in different districts. For example, in one district, the candidate pool consisted entirely of people who had successfully completed the preservice preparation program. That district reported devoting no resources to screening for the candidate pool. As another example, resources devoted to recruiting candidates tended to be lower in districts using a "grow your own" approach and higher for districts that were actively seeking candidates from outside the district.

Figure 3.8 presents information on the average spending on selective hiring and placement by year. As illustrated in Figure 3.8, average spending on selective hiring and placement increased about threefold in the first year of the initiative over our pre-initiative estimates, increased again in the second year of the initiative, and then began to decline. Four of the five districts included in our analysis of the selective hiring and placement component experienced a rise in costs from 2011–2012 to 2012–2013, with particularly large rises in two districts, both of which increased their spending on activities related to revision of hiring and placement, including the involvement of

Figure 3.7
Average Annual Per-Principal Resources and Expenditures for Hiring Activities, School Years 2011–2012 Through 2014–2015

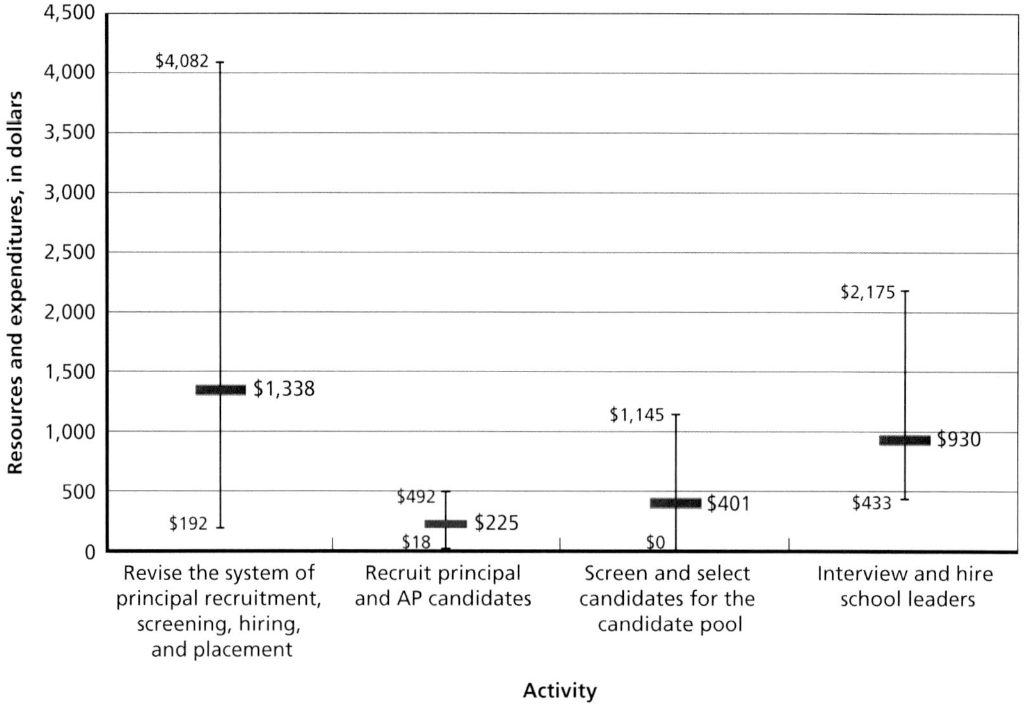

NOTE: We based estimates on average principal pipeline resources and expenditures across the five Principal Pipeline Initiative districts for which we had data for selective hiring and placement activities (i.e., excludes New York City).

RAND *RR2078-3.7*

more district personnel in hiring and placement revision processes and additional consultants to help assess and further develop recruitment and hiring strategies.

The predicted range of costs for 2015–2016 was very small ($2,031 to 2,083), which reflects that personnel made up 95 percent of the resources and expenditures for hiring activities in 2015–2016. Thus, the predicted range of resources and expenditures for 2015–2016—which compares doubled costs for the first half of 2015–2016 with costs that were doubled only for personnel who worked on hiring activities in the first half of 2015–2016—was also very small. Personnel costs made up 70 percent of the annual average spending for hiring activities from 2011–2012 to 2014–2015. Within these general trends, one district was consistently on the low end of spending on this component, and two districts were consistently on the higher end. Regardless of where they fell, all districts made investments to improve their hiring processes during the initiative.

Figure 3.8
Average Per-Principal Resources and Expenditures, by Year, for Hiring Activities

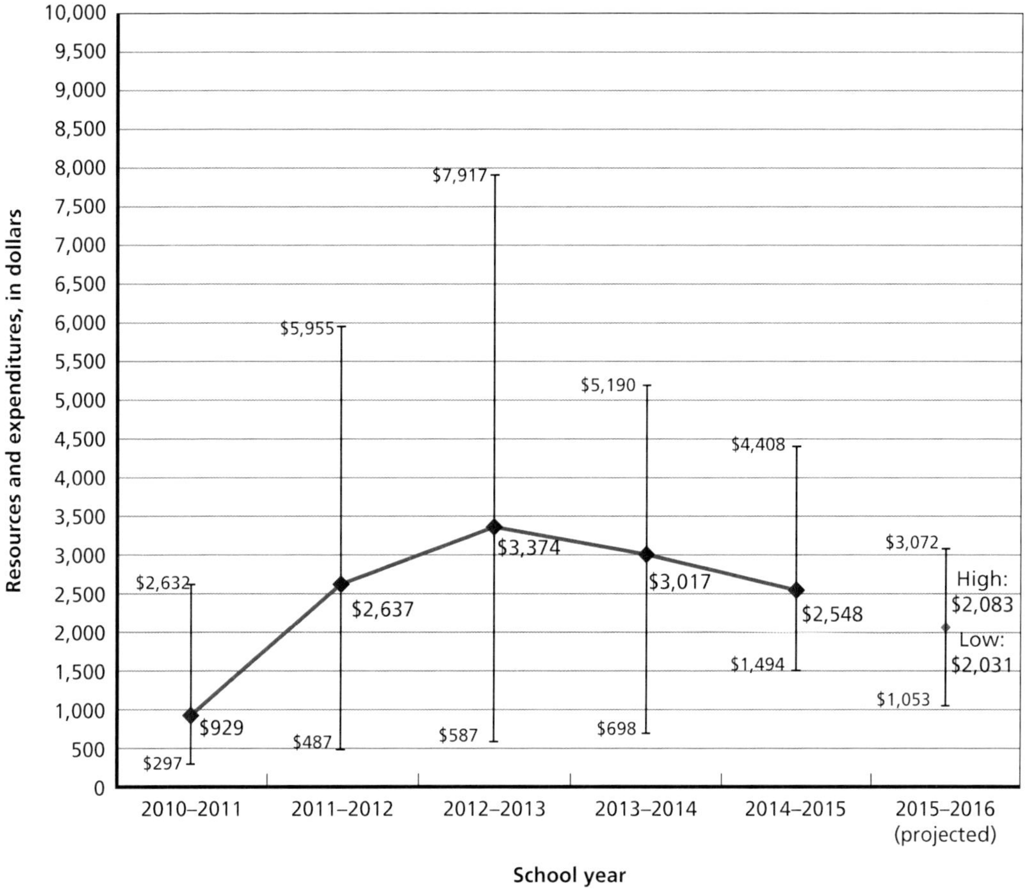

NOTE: We based estimates on average principal pipeline resources and expenditures across the five Principal Pipeline Initiative districts for which we had data for selective hiring and placement activities (i.e., excludes New York City).

RAND *RR2078-3.8*

Resources and Expenditures Devoted to Component 4: On-the-Job Support and Evaluation

Resources devoted to on-the-job support and evaluation include the resources involved in evaluating principals and APs, providing on-the-job support for them, and revising support and evaluation systems for them. Surveys suggest that new principals viewed the principal-evaluation systems favorably and appreciated the one-on-one mentoring, coaching, and on-the-job support provided by principal supervisors (Turnbull, Anderson, et al., 2016, pp. 37–47).[2]

All participating districts undertook efforts to align their school leaders' on-the-job support and evaluation systems with leader standards, and districts also considered how to provide professional learning and improvement opportunities that better aligned with their evaluation systems. As a part of this work, all districts took measures to improve principal supervision, and several districts expanded access to principal and AP coaching and mentoring. All districts used the SAM process to help school leaders increase time spent on instructional-leadership activities and improve effects on teaching and learning. Districts differed in terms of the mix of school leader supports they provided, as well as the intensity and duration of those supports. For example, one district developed an induction program that provided a structured sequence of support for novice principals over five years. Other districts focused on supporting principals in the first year or two.

Box 3.5 summarizes the main takeaways from our analysis of pipeline cost information related to on-the-job support and evaluation.

On average, across districts and across years, participating districts devoted $13,956 per principal or $18.53 per pupil to on-the-job support and evaluation activities. Figure 3.9 shows the average spending devoted to on-the-job support and evaluation, by year, during the initiative. Resources devoted to on-the-job support and evaluation varied substantially, both across districts and within districts over time, but to a lesser degree than we observed with preservice preparation. The average for the lowest-

Box 3.5

Key Takeaways: Resources Devoted to On-the-Job Support and Evaluation

- On average, districts devoted nearly half of total pipeline resources to on-the-job support and evaluation (47 percent), which amounted to $13,956 per principal or $18.53 per pupil.
- The vast majority of these resources were devoted to the provision of on-the-job support for principals and APs, including SAM. Districts devoted about $10,942 per principal to these activities, and on-the-job support was the most expensive activity of all principal pipeline activities across participating districts.
- Expenditures for on-the-job support included coaching and mentoring, principal supervision, the SAM process, costs for consultants, and the materials and supplies necessary for delivering ongoing PD for school leaders.

---

[2] As discussed in Turnbull, Anderson, et al., 2016, participating districts used the terms *coaching* and *mentoring* to refer to individualized support or guidance provided to aspiring or current leaders. In this report, we do not distinguish between mentoring and coaching and use the term *mentoring and coaching* to refer to this broad category of support.

Figure 3.9
Average Per-Principal Resources and Expenditures, by Year, for Support and Evaluation Activities

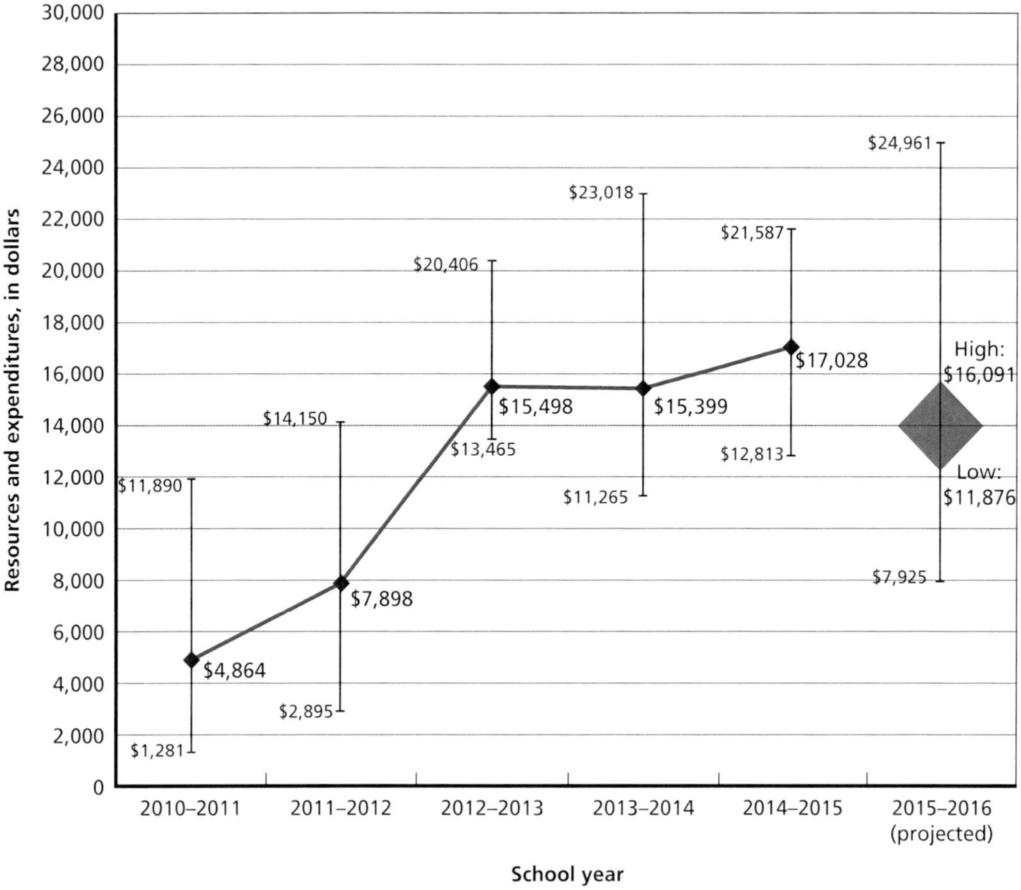

NOTE: We based estimates on average principal pipeline expenditures across the five Principal Pipeline Initiative districts for which we had data for on-the-job support and evaluation activities (i.e., excludes New York City).

RAND *RR2078-3.9*

spending district was $10,903 per principal, and the average for the highest-spending district was $19,790 per principal. All districts increased the resources devoted to on-the-job support and evaluation during the initiative, and the resources did not seem to be declining substantially as the initiative was winding down. Expenditures for on-the-job support and evaluation did appear to be related to the number of principals in the district. Districts with more principals tended to have higher expenditures in this category of activity, although other factors related to districts' starting points and strategies for preparing and supporting principals appeared to play a role as well.

The largest increase in costs for the on-the-job support and evaluation occurred from 2011–2012 to 2012–2013, when spending jumped by about $8,000 per principal, or $1.3 million on average, across participating districts. That is the largest year-to-year increase in spending for any pipeline component. The increase was not driven by any one district; all five districts for which we estimated costs of on-the-job support and evaluation saw large increases in costs for that component between 2011–2012 and 2012–2013. These increased costs were mostly due to large rises in the costs of on-the-job support for school leaders and—in the case of two districts—more spending for executive coaching as well. Average costs for on-the-job support and evaluation rose by a much smaller amount—about $1,600 per principal—between 2013–2014 and 2014–2015 because of rises in spending in three districts.

Figure 3.10 shows the average spending, by activity. As illustrated in Figure 3.10, the vast majority of resources directed toward this component were devoted to the provision of on-the-job support, including SAM support ($10,942 per principal per year, on average). In contrast, districts devoted only $1,385 per principal on average to principal and AP evaluation. Although all districts engaged in efforts to revise both evaluation systems and systems for on-the-job support, those reform efforts consumed relatively few resources. Over the course of the initiative, districts devoted an average of $513 per principal to revise their systems of providing on-the-job support and $381 per principal to revise systems for evaluation. They also devoted $734 per principal to provide executive coaching to those supporting leaders. As a reminder, the costs reported here on a per-principal basis are averaged over the total number of principals in a district, not the number who participate in a particular type of support activity.

A 2015 study by The New Teacher Project indicated that districts spend between $10,000 and $26,000 per teacher and between 5 and 10 percent of all district expenditures just on teacher PD (akin to what we define as on-the-job support for principals). Although PD expenditures are comparable on a per-teacher or per-principal basis, teacher PD consumes a much larger share of district spending because there are many more teachers than principals in a school district.

Not only was the delivery of on-the-job support for principals and APs the most costly activity in the fourth component of the pipeline (on-the-job support and evaluation); it was also the activity with the greatest cost across the entire principal pipeline. Given the high costs for delivery of on-the-job supports for school leaders, we investigated this activity in more detail. This investigation revealed several important takeaways. First, costs for principal on-the-job support made up a little more than 70 percent of the annual average cost for on-the-job school leader support overall ($6,411 per principal, annually), whereas AP on-the-job support made up only about 20 percent of all on-the-job support costs. If SAM support is also included as principal on-the-job support, the percentage of on-the-job support for principals swells to 77 percent of the total costs of on-the-job support for school leaders. More-generalized school support—which could assist both principals and APs—made up a little less than 10 percent of the total costs for on-the-job school leader support.

Figure 3.10
Average Annual Per-Principal Resources and Expenditures for Support and Evaluation Activities, School Years 2011–2012 Through 2014–2015

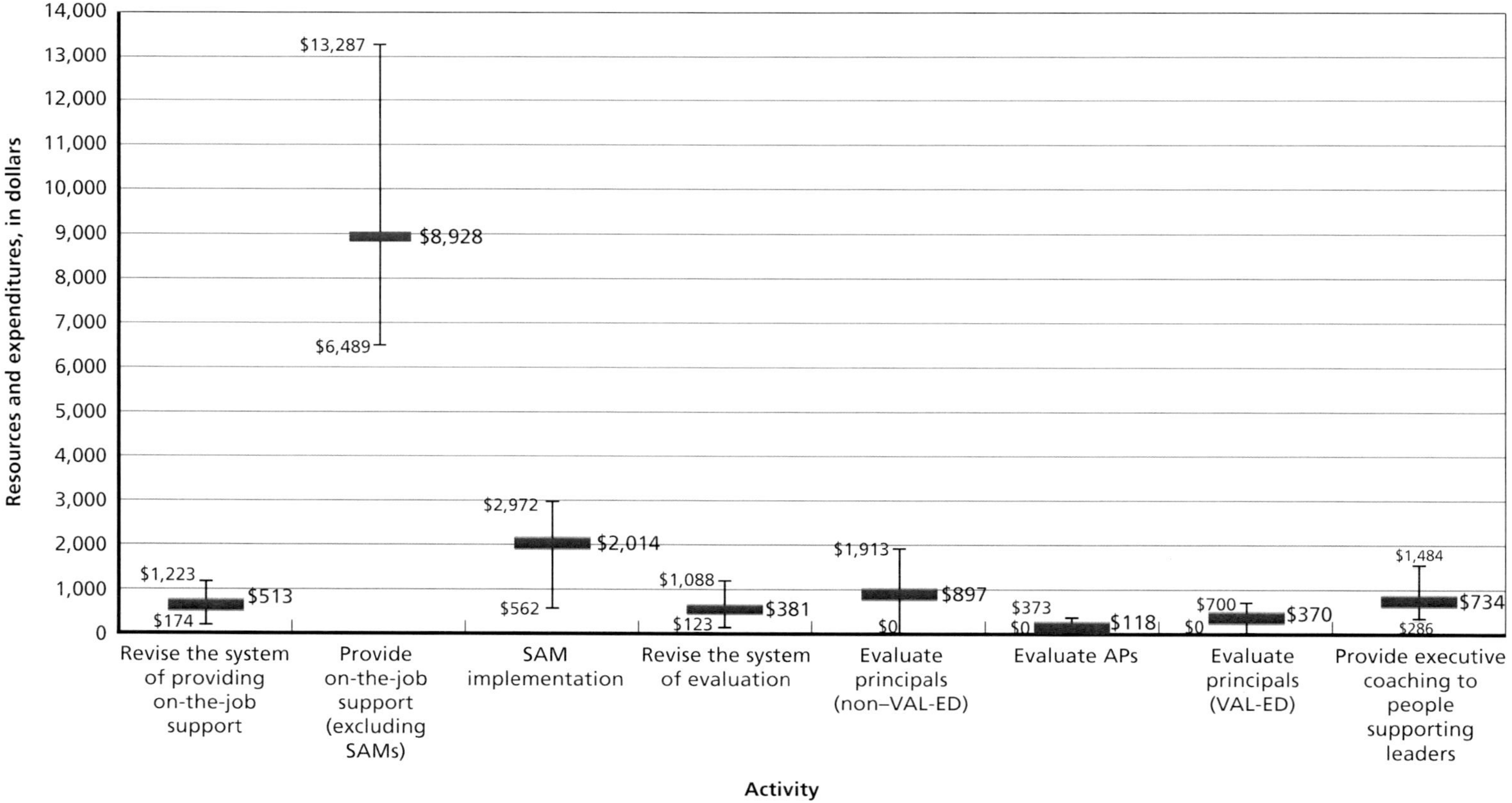

NOTE: We based estimates on average principal pipeline expenditures across the five Principal Pipeline Initiative districts for which we had data for on-the-job support and evaluation activities (i.e., excludes New York City).

RAND *RR2078-3.10*

The costs for on-the-job support for principals and APs were somewhat varied across districts, although some substantial portion of that cost in every district was a general line item for "principal professional development/PD," which—according to the districts—was a line item covering the costs of all materials, supplies, travel, and consultants supporting principal PD. In addition, the cost of principal supervisor time to provide on-the-job support was relatively high. Specifically, principal supervisors generally spent about 15 percent of their time on on-the-job support for principals during and after the first year, on average, including support for SAMs. In addition, salaries and stipends for principal and AP coaching and mentoring amounted to about $1,500 per principal, on average over all principals, annually. Thus, the cost of coaching and mentoring represented more than 10 percent of the total on-the-job support costs. Other on-the-job support costs that were included in some districts included the costs for specific PD institutes, support for principals and APs in struggling or high-needs schools, and costs of HR staff who served specific schools and supported principal on-boarding.

Resources and Expenditures Devoted to Systems and Capacity for Supporting Pipeline Components

Each of the participating districts also devoted staff and other resources to four activities that cut across the four initiative components. Those activities included efforts to revise the principal pipeline, oversee the implementation of pipeline activities, develop and maintain LTSs, and engage in communication about the pipeline. According to an informal survey conducted by The Wallace Foundation, the vast majority of district officials in all participating districts indicated that they found the LTSs to be worthwhile or very worthwhile (Gill, 2016), although this finding could reflect a desire on the part of initiative participants to tell the funder something positive about a key aspect of the initiative. Over the course of the initiative, districts devoted $3,425 per principal on average annually—or an average of $672,252 per year—toward these four activities. The average annual per-principal costs for pipeline systems of support in one district were substantially lower than in other districts ($176). Average annual per-principal resources and expenditures in the other districts ranged from $3,395 to $5,406 per principal per year.

Box 3.6 summarizes the main takeaways from our analysis of pipeline cost information related to systems of support. Figure 3.11 describes the average annual per-principal resources and expenditures for systems of support activities over time during the initiative. Although the overall resources dedicated to systems of support were stable over time, there was variation from year to year within each district. This is reflected in Figure 3.11 by the wide range of average costs each year and, particularly, at the start of the initiative in 2011–2012. For the most part, districts devoted very

Box 3.6

Key Takeaways: Resources Devoted to Systems of Support

- The development and maintenance of LTSs were the largest drivers of costs for systems of support for principal pipeline components, at almost $2,000 per principal each year, on average.
- Spending on the LTSs over the course of the initiative was not related to any metric of district size.
- All districts invested at least some resources and expenditures in communications about the initiative, and most hired consultants or others to help them plan communication strategies and messaging about initiative efforts. All districts also invested resources in quality assurance of pipeline efforts.

few resources to these activities prior to the launch of the initiative. Preinitiative costs were represented mostly by a few district personnel who spent time thinking about and overseeing the entire pipeline of preparation, hiring, support, and evaluation for school leaders prior to the initiative.

Figure 3.12 describes the average annual per-principal resources and expenditures, by activity. Variation in the costs of this component during the initiative was driven by higher costs of LTS activities in certain years for some districts. Some districts devoted substantial resources to the LTSs early in the initiative, whereas others postponed these efforts until later. The LTS efforts accounted for about half of the resources devoted to systems of support (on average, nearly $400,000 per year or about $1,990 per principal per year). For leader tracking, one district had substantially lower costs on a per-principal basis than other districts (an average of $52 per principal per year); other districts devoted between $1,451 and $4,247 per principal per year (or between about $215,000 and just over $900,000 overall per year) to LTSs. Some of these leader tracking resources came to the districts in the form of technical assistance, which was paid for directly by The Wallace Foundation.

Total spending on the LTSs over the course of the initiative was not related to any metric of district size. Variation in spending for LTSs can be better explained, in part, by different starting points in different districts. Prior to receiving Wallace funding, participating districts had made diverse investments in technology that supported preparation, hiring, support, and evaluation for principals. For instance, some districts had already made at least some investments in systems that tracked school leader and teacher applicants. One district had purchased online PD modules for school leaders and teachers and tracked completion of those modules. Our estimates included the time of personnel who used these systems regularly to enter and maintain data, technical personnel who supported upgrades to these systems and could troubleshoot when problems arose, and any costs of updated software and hardware.

Figure 3.11
Average Per-Principal Resources and Expenditures, by Year, for Systems and Capacity Activities

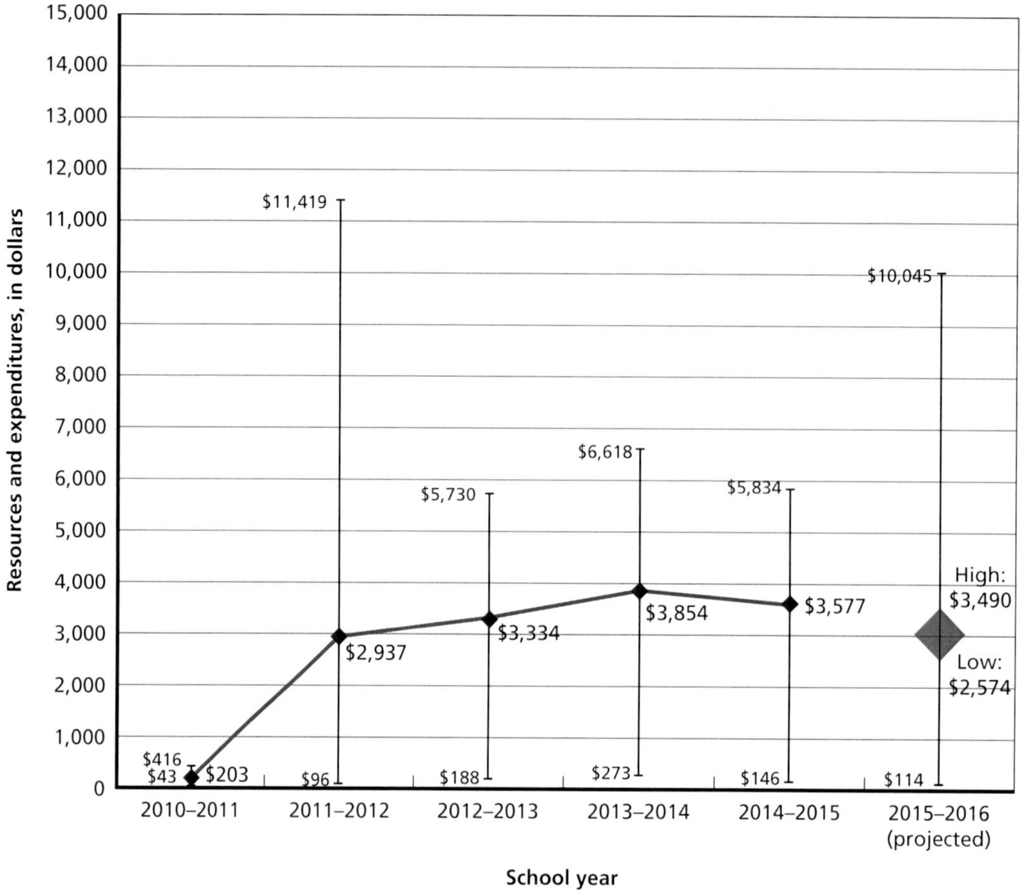

NOTE: We based estimates on average principal pipeline resources and expenditures across all Principal Pipeline Initiative districts.

RAND *RR2078-3.11*

All districts also committed at least some resources across years to develop and disseminate communication about the initiative ($608 per principal per year, on average). Some districts relied on district personnel, such as principal supervisors and principal pipeline managers, to provide that communication, although districts also worked with web designers and communication consultants to ensure that they were providing other district staff, school leaders, partners, and others with clear information about leader standards and their principal pipeline efforts.

Figure 3.12
Average Annual Per-Principal Resources and Expenditures for Systems and Capacity Activities, School Years 2011–2012 Through 2014–2015

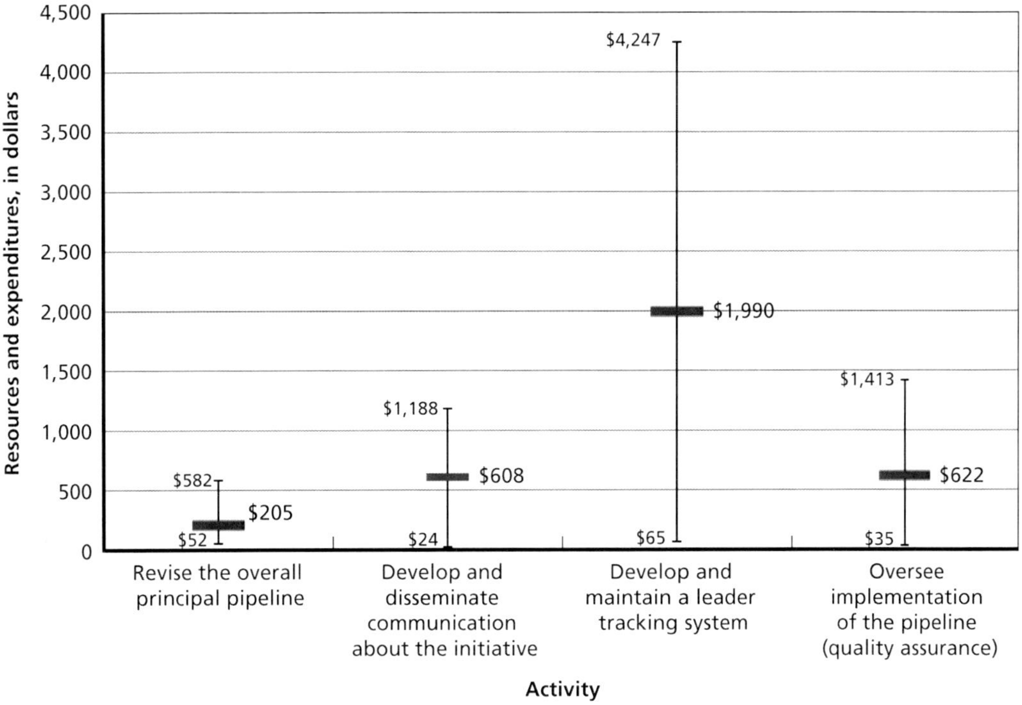

RAND *RR2078-3.12*

CHAPTER FOUR

Findings on Investments and Staffing Necessary for Pipeline Enhancements

The Principal Pipeline Initiative catalyzed districts to make investments in their pipelines. These investments in the pipelines were intended to support work to design, develop, and refine district systems. Investments were thus intended to support reflection and new approaches in all districts. All districts were expected to incur costs for these investments. The grants from The Wallace Foundation were expected to defray some of those investment costs while preparing districts to sustain ongoing pipeline activities on their own.

In this chapter, we consider what share of spending went to pipeline investments and what share focused on ongoing costs, as well as what share of the investment and ongoing costs were funded by The Wallace Foundation. We also take a closer look at what it takes to build and maintain comprehensive principal pipelines in terms of district personnel involved in pipeline activities, taking into account all personnel but also taking a closer look at the time that principal supervisors contribute to pipeline activities. In addition, we explore the costs associated with the time spent on pipeline activities by principals and APs who participated in those activities.

Investments in Pipeline Enhancements

There are two lenses through which to consider investment in pipeline enhancements and distinguish them from resources devoted to the ongoing operation of principal pipelines. One is to examine the resources devoted to pipeline activities that explicitly pertain to revision of the pipeline or development of new systems. These include the following activities that are part of the entire list of principal pipeline activities (see Table 2.1 in Chapter Two for the full list):

- Develop or revise leader standards and secure their approval.
- Revise the system of preservice recruitment, selection, and preparation.
- Revise the system for principal recruiting, hiring, and placement (design processes and train personnel).
- Revise the system for providing on-the-job support for principals and APs.

- Revise the system for providing evaluation for principals and APs.
- Revise the overall principal pipeline.
- Develop and disseminate communication about the initiative.
- Develop and maintain LTSs.

The average total per-principal expenditures for the activities listed above pertaining to pipeline revision or development of new systems were $7,108 per principal per year, ranging from a low of $5,676 in one district to a high of $9,732 in another district.[1]

The problem with this way of identifying investments as pipeline enhancement activities is that districts approached pipeline improvement by trying out new approaches and systems across multiple activities (Turnbull, Anderson, et al., 2016, p. 61). New strategies for implementing evaluation, on-the-job training, or preservice preparation were piloted in most districts. In some cases, pilots worked out well and the approach was incorporated into the districts' pipeline (possibly after some modification). In other cases, pilots revealed fundamental flaws with particular strategies, so those strategies were discarded. This pilot-testing was another form of investment. By the same token, districts viewed some efforts to revise key aspects of the pipeline (i.e., the activities described in the list above) not as one-time investments but rather as part of an ongoing continuous quality improvement process that would be sustained after the initiative ended (Turnbull, Anderson, et al., 2016, p. viii). For example, investments in revision of hiring and placement—or revision to any component—were not expected to cease entirely at the end of the initiative. District personnel planned to revisit and reflect on the pieces of their pipelines on a regular basis, drawing on data from LTSs, and revise pipeline categories accordingly.

Through substantial back and forth discussions with district points of contact, we worked to distinguish between resources devoted to pipeline investments and those for the ongoing operation of the pipeline in a way that addresses the concerns described above. To accomplish this aim, we leveraged information in expenditure reports that districts provided to The Wallace Foundation. In these reports, The Wallace Foundation asked districts to distinguish between expenditures related to "one-time" costs for investment and "ongoing" costs to sustain and maintain pipeline systems. In expenditure report requests, The Wallace Foundation instructed districts to consider "one-time" investment costs as "innovation and development costs that may be borne primarily by Wallace in a given time frame and sustained by the grantee subsequently through ongoing costs."[2] In our own work to categorize expenditures as investment or ongoing costs, we generally adhered to the determinations the districts had already

---

[1] We did not include New York City in these average calculations because we could not estimate costs for all activities included here.

[2] This was noted in informal expenditure report request documents that Wallace gave to districts.

made. However, district personnel costs were categorized as investment or ongoing costs based on the activities in which personnel were involved. Chapter Two and the appendix include more details on how we categorized investment and ongoing expenditures. However, readers should keep in mind that, given all participating districts' commitments to continuous quality improvement, resources devoted to "investment" in pipeline enhancement were not expected to disappear completely for any districts in the foreseeable future.[3]

As seen in Figure 4.1, districts considered 30 percent of district expenditures on the principal pipeline to be "investments" in pipeline enhancements, whereas 70 percent was dedicated to ongoing pipeline operation. The share of resources devoted to one-time investments did not vary a great deal across districts (19 percent at the low end and 38 percent at the high end). The districts with the most-developed principal pipelines at the start of the initiative did not necessarily invest less in their pipelines than those with the least developed ones. Instead, those with lower investments might not have chosen to make as many costly revisions to their pipelines over the course of the initiative as others did. Unsurprisingly, the major activities with the highest investment costs included those requiring substantial development and revision time and lower ongoing costs after development and revision took place. For example, leader standards was the category with the highest percentage of total resources devoted to investment, whereas selective hiring and placement had the lowest share of expenditures devoted to investment.

A relatively high share of resources devoted to systems and capacity for supporting the initiative were characterized as investments rather than ongoing pipeline operations, especially when it came to LTSs. Sixty-three percent of the resources devoted to LTSs were considered to be investments.

Although a relatively low share of resources devoted to hiring and placement overall were investments, we were able to identify some specific activities within the hiring and placement category for which a large share of spending was considered to be investments. For example, districts considered 61 percent of the average annual resources devoted to the revision of hiring and placement to be investments.[4] Districts varied in the extent to which they viewed resources associated with hiring system revi-

---

[3] Ideally, we would have liked to treat investment costs in a more rigorous way by estimating the life span of the investments and allocating the costs incurred in one SY across that estimated life span. That was not possible to do for this study because of the nature of the investment expenditures, none of which were capital assets of that sort (e.g., building purchases). The "assets" in which participating districts were investing were processes that have unknown or even flexible life spans. Although we did ask district officials to think about how often they might repeat certain investment activities, district officials could not provide concrete estimates and indicated that the time frame would depend on a variety of factors.

[4] One might think that the entirety of spending involved in the revision of systems would be viewed as investments. However, participating districts viewed some system revision activities as an inherent part of continuous quality improvement processes. As a result, all districts reported that at least some share of the system revision costs should be considered operation rather than investment spending.

Figure 4.1
Investment and Ongoing Resources and Expenditures, Overall and by Major Category, Based on Analyses from School Years 2011–2012 Through 2014–2015

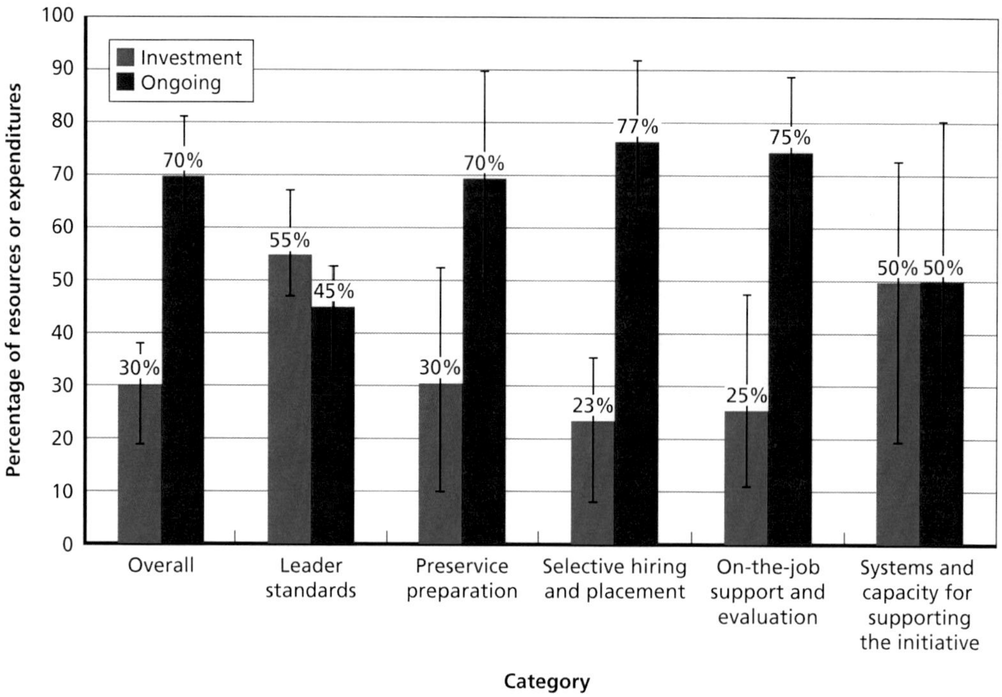

NOTE: We based overall percentage estimates and those for the selective hiring and placement and on-the-job support and evaluation activities on investment and ongoing resources and expenditures across the five Principal Pipeline Initiative districts for which we had those data (i.e., excludes New York City). The error bars represent the range from the district with the lowest percentage of investment and ongoing costs for each component to the district with the highest percentage of investment and ongoing costs.

RAND *RR2078-4.1*

sion to be an investment rather than an ongoing cost. In one district, nearly 90 percent of the costs for revision of hiring and placement were characterized as investments, compared with just one-quarter of all costs in another district.

As indicated in Figure 4.2, the percentage of total costs that the districts characterized as investments was highest in 2012–2013 and then steadily decreased through 2014–2015, increasing slightly in 2015–2016.[5] The greatest variation across districts in terms of the share of costs characterized as investment was evident at the beginning of the initiative, which is perhaps unsurprising, given that all the districts began the initiative with very different systems and needs for supporting and improving their principal pipelines.

---

[5] The percentage of investment and ongoing costs for 2015–2016 is based only on pipeline costs for the first six months of 2015–2016. The slight rise in percentage of investment costs represented in the figure might not reflect spending for the entirety of 2015–2016.

Figure 4.2
Investment and Ongoing Resources and Expenditures, by Year

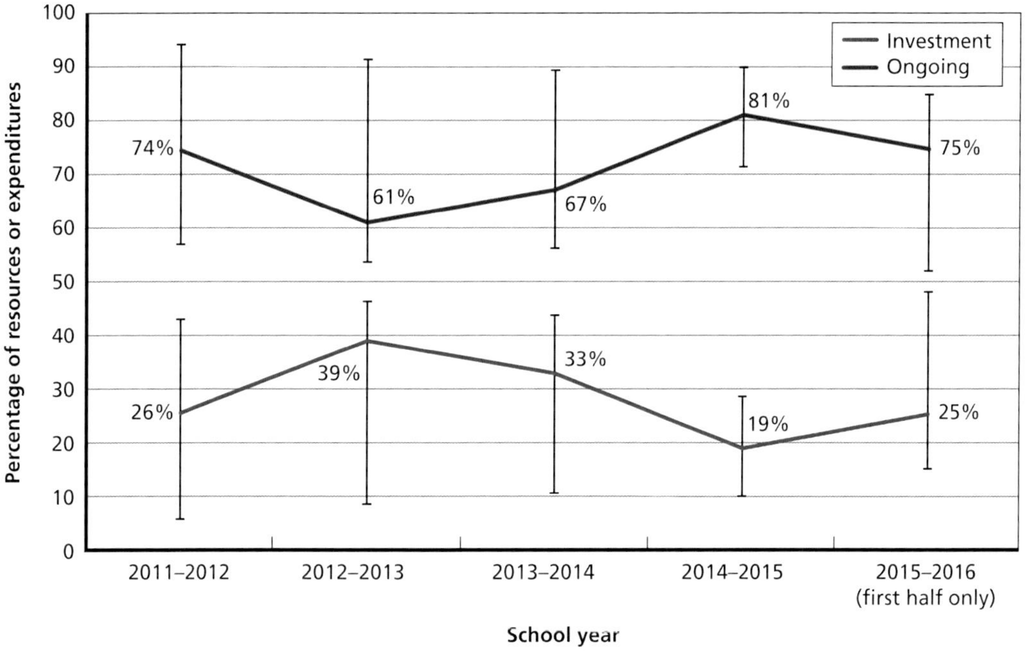

NOTE: We based percentage estimates on investment and ongoing resources and expenditures across the five Principal Pipeline Initiative districts for which we had data for all pipeline costs (i.e., excludes New York City).
RAND *RR2078-4.2*

What Role Did Funding from The Wallace Foundation Play?

Other districts considering whether to undertake efforts to enhance their principal pipelines might wonder what role the funding from The Wallace Foundation played in the overall pipeline efforts. In this section, we describe our efforts to characterize how the districts used funding from The Wallace Foundation. The Wallace Foundation provided funds for each district's pipeline work, ranging from $7.5 million to $12.5 million over five years. The foundation expected that districts would also devote their own resources to principal pipelines, reflecting the fact that operating principal pipelines is a district responsibility. All districts used funds from a range of other sources beyond The Wallace Foundation to support their pipeline efforts. For example, many districts reported using several sources of federal funding—e.g., Race to the Top, Title II, and the Teacher Incentive Fund—to support principal effectiveness efforts and support principals in the most-struggling schools. Most districts also noted receiving foundation funding to support specific aspects of their principal pipeline efforts, such as a particular leader development program or technology to support leader tracking.

In addition, districts used state and local funds for salaries and stipends of personnel supporting school leadership, among other, more-routine costs.

The grants from The Wallace Foundation to the districts were structured in such a way as to encourage districts to take on a larger percentage of the total cost of their pipelines over time. In their expenditure reports to The Wallace Foundation, districts indicated which expenditures the foundation funded. They were also asked to report on pipeline expenditures funded by district funds and other sources. The expenditure reports provided a fairly comprehensive picture of the share of pipeline activities covered by Wallace funds, although those expenditure reports did not include all of the resources and expenditures that we gathered through our study and thus provided a less comprehensive picture of the non-Wallace spending.

We calculated the percentage of total costs funded by Wallace by taking the Wallace-funded expenditures that the districts reported for each year—plus the expenditures associated with technical assistance provided by external providers to the district that The Wallace Foundation funded directly[6]—and dividing it by the total pipeline costs we calculated for that year for the district.

As seen in Figure 4.3, the percentage of pipeline expenditures that funds from The Wallace Foundation supported was highest in 2012–2013. Over the course of the initiative, the portion of the total funding that Wallace contributed steadily decreased to 27 percent in 2015–2016. The range of expenditures that Wallace supported also steadily decreased over time. Thus, toward the end of the initiative, the portion of each district's total funding that Wallace supported was more similar to the portion that Wallace supported in the earliest years of the initiative.

As we noted earlier, Wallace support was intended to fund mostly investment costs. In our analysis, we attempted to distinguish between activities that Wallace supported and non-Wallace funds based on reports that districts submitted to The Wallace Foundation. Because district resources are highly fungible, we urge caution in interpreting findings about the source of funding. Districts might have reported using more of the Wallace funding on investment costs but in actuality did not have that much control over what Wallace funding paid for. As seen in Figure 4.4, Wallace Foundation funds supported a majority of the expenditures that districts characterized as investments. On average, about two-thirds of investment in pipeline enhancements across districts was supported by The Wallace Foundation, compared with just 20 percent of the ongoing pipeline operation spending. Although the portion of each district's pipeline spending that The Wallace Foundation supported decreased over time overall, the portion of districts' investments in pipeline enhancements that Wallace supported fluctuated somewhat over the course of the initiative. Specifically, Wallace Founda-

---

[6] The technical assistance costs we included were those costs that both The Wallace Foundation and the districts agreed provided essential and important support for particular pipeline activities. The Wallace Foundation provided us with separate expenditure reports for the technical assistance providers.

Figure 4.3
Percentage of Resources and Expenditures That The Wallace Foundation Funded in Each Year

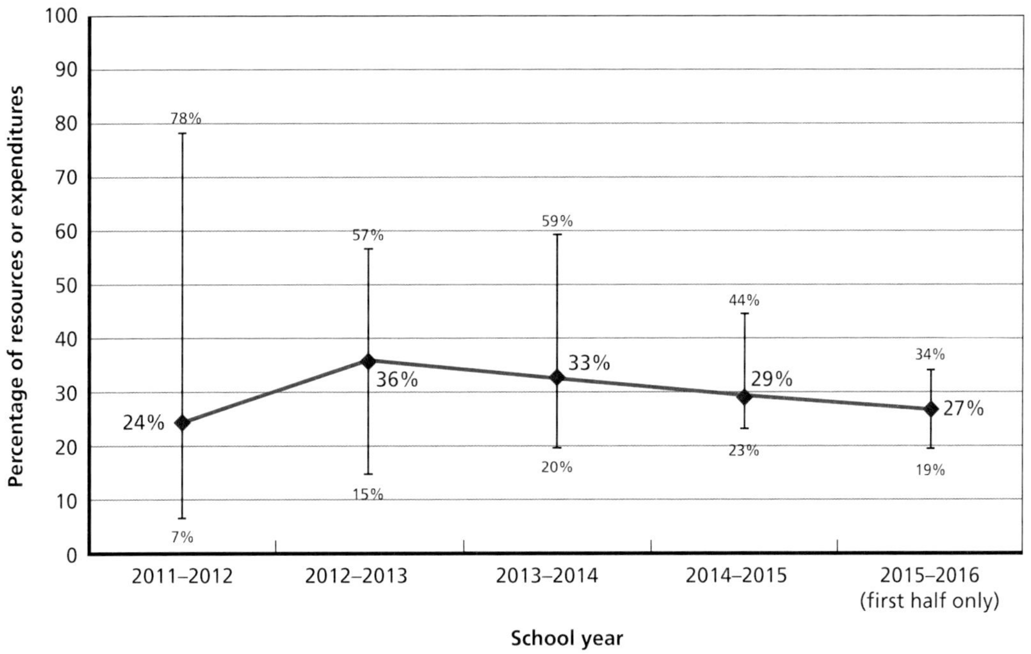

NOTE: We based percentage estimates on Wallace and non-Wallace resources and expenditures across the five Principal Pipeline Initiative districts for which we had data for all pipeline costs (i.e., excludes New York City).

RAND *RR2078-4.3*

tion support for investments started out high at the beginning of the initiative and then decreased through 2013–2014. However, in 2014–2015, the share of investment expenditures that Wallace funds supported increased to a high of nearly 80 percent, then decreased again in the following year. Although Wallace funds supported a larger share of investments in pipeline enhancements in 2014–2015, the total investment expenditures in each district decreased in that year. Thus, the total investment funding that Wallace provided in 2014–2015 increased by only about $500,000 from 2013–2014 to 2014–2015 despite a large jump in the percentage of investment expenditures that Wallace funds covered.

District Personnel Time on Principal Pipeline Activities

Some portion of the cost for every principal pipeline activity is cost for the time and work of district staff, even keeping in mind that we did not include the time of principals and APs in our cost estimates. As described in Chapter Two and the appendix, we calculated

Figure 4.4
Percentage of Resources and Expenditures That The Wallace Foundation Funded, by Investment and Ongoing

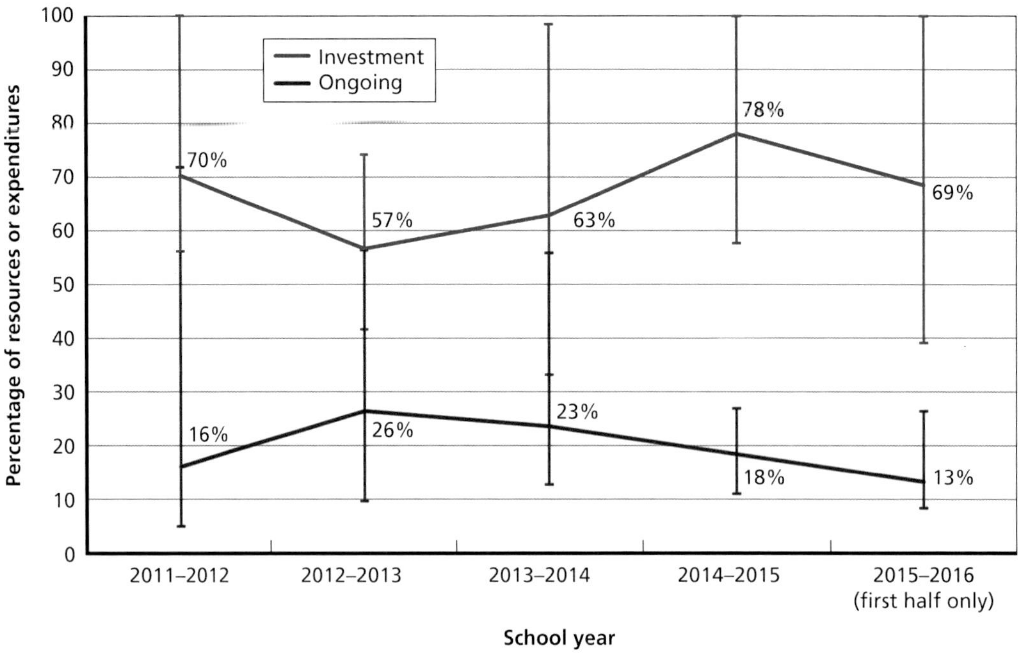

NOTE: We based percentage estimates on Wallace and non-Wallace resources and expenditures across the five Principal Pipeline Initiative districts for which we had data for all pipeline costs (i.e., excludes New York City).

RAND *RR2078-4.4*

the cost of that time by asking personnel to estimate the percentage of their time spent on various pipeline activities and allocating that percentage of their salary and benefits to those activities. For this section, we discuss personnel costs in more depth.[7] Box 4.1 summarizes key takeaways related to expenditures related to the time of district personnel.

Table 4.1 summarizes the resources that participating districts devoted to district personnel expenditures and their share of total pipeline expenditures. On average, the cost of district personnel time devoted to the principal pipeline amounted to about \$13,045 per principal, or \$2.42 million, per year across all pipeline activities. District personnel time accounted for an average of 44 percent of the resources devoted to all pipeline activities over the course of the initiative, although the time of district personnel played a bigger role in some activities than others. District personnel time accounted for 84 percent of the resources devoted to work on leader standards. In each

[7] As a reminder, we did *not* consider supplemental payments to principals or APs as part of personnel costs because we wanted to provide districts with clear information about what it takes in terms of personnel to support and direct pipeline work.

Box 4.1

Key Takeaways: Expenditures Associated with District Personnel Time

- Costs of district personnel made up nearly half, or about 44 percent, of all the costs for pipeline activities.
- District personnel time accounted for a particularly large portion of the total resources devoted to leader standard development and all hiring and placement activities.
- Expenditures associated with the cost of district personnel time were highest for on-the-job support and evaluation activities. Principal supervisors, as well as other district personnel, contributed to these support and evaluation activities.
- During the initiative, all districts increased supervisory time on pipeline activities by increasing the number of principal supervisors overall or decreasing the time that principal supervisors spent on non–pipeline-related activities.
- Novice principals and APs likely spent high percentages of their time on some aspects of pipeline activities, including their own PD, but that time might have enhanced their work on other priorities more than it hindered that work.

Table 4.1
Share of Pipeline Expenditures That Were District Personnel Expenditures

	Per-Principal Expenditures, in Dollars		Percentage of Expenditures for District Personnel
Average Across Districts	Total	District Personnel	
Leader standards	292	244	84
Preservice recruitment, selection, and training	9,386	2,499	23
Selective hiring and placement	2,894	1,716	69
On-the-job support and evaluation	13,956	6,465	44
Systems and capacity for supporting the initiative	3,425	1,457	47

NOTE: The percentage of spending for district personnel for each major category in the table is the average of the percentage of spending for personnel in each district and not the result of dividing personnel expenditures by total expenditures for each category. Average estimates for the selective hiring and placement and on-the-job support and evaluation activities take into account only the five initiative districts for which we had those data (i.e., excludes New York City).

district, anywhere between four and 11 people contributed at least some small portion of their time to work on the development of leader standards in any given year. Those people generally included the key people overseeing the principal pipelines in their districts, as well as personnel in various other key positions related to the pipelines, including, for example, those who supervise principals and those directing principal PD, principal evaluation, or district-led preparation programs. Some districts also included a small number of principals and APs on the committees that discussed the development and revision of leader standards.

In contrast, district personnel time played a less substantial role in preservice preparation.[8] Personnel time for preservice preparation was directed to such activities as recruitment for preservice programs, as well as screening and selecting preservice preparation candidates. The cost of district personnel time made up almost one-quarter of the cost of preservice preparation delivery and was concentrated in the costs of district-led preservice preparation programs.

On-the-job support and evaluation consumed the most district personnel time of all major categories—nearly $6,500 per principal, or 44 percent of the total cost for on-the-job support and evaluation. This is because districts provided many on-the-job support and evaluation activities themselves, with less support from contractors and other providers than preservice preparation had. In fact, personnel costs made up 51 percent of the costs for the delivery of on-the-job support activity across districts, and the costs for district personnel made up 56 percent of the cost of evaluating principals and APs.

Principal Supervisors

As noted in Turnbull, Anderson, et al., 2016, part of the principal pipeline work involved redefining the role of principal supervisors, with a focus on increasing the time that principal supervisors spent advising and supporting principals and reducing time on administrative and compliance tasks. Our cost analyses provide some insights regarding changes to principal supervision over the course of the initiative.[9] First, as also noted in Turnbull, Anderson, et al., 2016, our analysis indicates that the number of principal supervisors increased over time in three districts and—thus, given the stability in the number of principals in each district over time—the "span of control" or numbers of principals that a single supervisor oversaw decreased over time, on average. In those three districts, the average number of principals that a single supervisor oversaw in 2010–2011 was 28 principals, compared with an average number of 14 principals overseen by a single supervisor in 2015–2016. Two districts—one where the span of control changed and one where it did not—also reported that principal supervisors

[8] As discussed earlier, a large portion of preservice costs were payments for principal and AP residencies, which we do not consider personnel costs for the purpose of this reporting.

[9] Our analyses of principal supervisor time and cost do not include New York City.

spent more time overall on pipeline activities than on administrative or compliance duties unrelated to the principal pipeline.

Table 4.2 presents information on the average percentage of time that principal supervisors spent on each major category of pipeline activity during the initiative, as well as information on the minimum and maximum percentages of time spent in a district. In reviewing these findings, it is important to keep in mind that principal supervisors typically had district responsibilities beyond the principal pipeline and devoted only a fraction of their time to pipeline activities. Although districts worked to reduce the span of control among supervisors and increased time on pipeline activities in general, the manner in which supervisors allocated their time *among* pipeline activities changed very little over the course of the initiative. Most supervisors spent time on the same activities in each year, although the percentage of their time spent on those activities also increased somewhat in the two districts where supervisors reportedly spent more time on the pipeline in general.

Supervisors spent at least some time on a similar set of pipeline activities across districts within the major categories in Table 4.2. In particular, all supervisors spent at least some time on principal interviewing activities (a little more than 5 percent of their time, on average). Principal interviewing is one activity in component 3 (selective hiring and placement). As seen in Table 4.2, the activities in component 4 (on-the-job support and evaluation) took up 22 percent of supervisors' time (the most of any principal pipeline activity). In this component, supervisors dedicated—on average—more than 12 percent of their time to on-the-job support for principals in and beyond their first year, although they contributed less than 5 percent of their time to supporting APs in and beyond their first year. In addition, supervisors spent about 6 percent of their time, on average, on principal evaluation. Beyond those four activities (principal interviewing, on-the-job support for first-year principals, on-the-job support for principals after the first year, and principal evaluation), there was variation in the activities on which supervisors spent their time. In three districts, supervisors spent a small percentage of their time on preservice

Table 4.2
Average Percentage of Time That Supervisors Spent on Pipeline Activities

	Percentage of Time Spent on Pipeline Activities		
Category	**Average**	**Minimum**	**Maximum**
Leader standards	2.5	0.0	11.7
Preservice recruitment, selection, and training	1.3	0.0	3.9
Selective hiring and placement	6.4	1.9	16.1
On-the-job support and evaluation	21.8	2.5	58.9
Systems and capacity for supporting the initiative	0.6	0.0	1.3

NOTE: Percentage estimates are based on averages across the five participating districts for which we have data on supervisory time across all pipeline activities (i.e., excludes New York City).

preparation activities, including activities that might range from work on the revision of preservice preparation to screening and recruitment for preservice preparation and some participation in the delivery. In two districts, principal supervisors spent time providing on-the-job support for APs in addition to principals. In two districts, supervisors spent a very small portion of their time weighing in on revisions to the entire principal pipeline or communicating with others about the Principal Pipeline Initiative.

Turnbull, Anderson, et al., 2016, notes that principal supervisors "took on pivotal roles in on the job evaluation and support" (p. 37). This finding is consistent with the findings from our resource analysis. Although districts' reports indicate that individual principal supervisors did not substantially alter the way they allocated their time among pipeline activities, they did indicate that principal supervisors spent a higher percentage of their total time, on average, on on-the-job support and evaluation than on any other major category. Furthermore, principals and APs would have likely received more attention from principal supervisors—especially in terms of on-the-job support and evaluation—over the course of the initiative, given that principal supervisor span of control decreased in three districts and principal supervisors increased their time spent on all pipeline activities in two districts.

Districts that are reflecting about the best way to increase supervisor time on principal pipeline activities could thus follow one of the two strategies followed by participating districts: Increase the number of principal supervisors, or determine ways to offload work on nonpipeline activities to other personnel. The former strategy could seem more expensive to implement than the latter, given that it would require paying salaries for more principal supervisors. On the other hand, pursuing the latter strategy would require districts to identify and train other district personnel to take on more administrative tasks previously taken on by the principal supervisor. In our data-collection work, we could not document the potential "costs" of the latter strategy, but such costs—particularly in terms of opportunity costs and costs of time for training and support—could be considerable. On the other hand, participating districts reported that reorganizing the role of principal supervisor could be accomplished in a revenue-neutral manner as part of a broader assessment of central office roles.

Time That Principals and Assistant Principals Spent on Pipeline Activities

Although we did not include principal and AP time on principal pipeline activities in our cost estimates, that time can be regarded as an opportunity cost. Participating districts asked principals and APs to contribute many hours of their time, not only to their own PD but also to supporting the PD of others through formal mentoring and coaching activities, as well as other pipeline categories, such as leader standard development and hiring.[10]

---

[10] School leaders were sometimes paid small stipends to serve as mentors, and we did count those expenditures in our estimates of principal pipeline costs. But if the cost of such mentoring is calculated as the portion of prin-

Figure 4.5 captures the average percentage of time that novice principals and APs—those in their first three years on the job—reported spending on selected principal pipeline activities in a survey fielded in participating districts in each of two calendar years: 2014 and 2015. As can be seen in the figure, novice principals reported spending a fairly large percentage of their time—about 19 percent, on average, in 2014 and 2015—participating in their own PD activities. On average, in 2014 and 2015, principals also reported spending 7 percent of their time mentoring or coaching aspiring or current school leaders, 2 percent on screening and hiring of other school leaders, and 5 percent evaluating other school leaders. Taking into account the average principal salary in each district, the cost of principal time on these activities would be about $33,730 per principal, or about $6.3 million annually. The cost of those activities based on reports of APs would be about $33,160 per AP, or about $12.2 million annually.

The average percentage time estimates that novice principals and APs provided are likely not representative of all principals and APs across participating districts. For example, the time spent on PD could be much higher among novice principals and APs than all principals, whereas the time spent on mentoring or coaching of other school leaders is likely to be much lower among newer school leaders. In addition, the percentage time estimates decreased significantly for PD from 2014 to 2015 among both principals and APs and for mentoring among principals, which could reflect adjustments that districts made in how much they asked of school leaders over time.

The time and effort that school leaders devote to pipeline activities could be particularly characterized as a cost to school districts if they take time away from other important priorities that school leaders have in their schools or districts. This cost of principal and AP time could thus be regarded as an opportunity cost, or the benefit that the district could have received but gave up to focus on principal pipeline activities.[11] The PSA survey asked novice principals and APs whether the time they spent on the principal pipeline prevented them from attending to other important school priorities, as well as whether it enhanced their ability to attend to important school priorities.

Table 4.3 summarizes some additional key survey findings. Only 7.5 percent of principals and 10 percent of APs agreed that it hindered their ability to attend to other school priorities, whereas more than one-quarter of principals and more than one-third of APs indicated that it enhanced that ability. This limited survey evidence, based on surveys of new principals and APs, suggests that pipeline activities might have a low opportunity cost, at least in the eyes of school leaders.

---

cipal and AP salaries based on the percentage of time that they actually spent on mentoring activities, the cost of mentoring could exceed those stipends.

[11] For a definition of opportunity cost, see "Opportunity Cost," undated.

Figure 4.5
Average Percentage of Time That Novice Principals and Assistant Principals Reported Spending on Principal Pipeline Activities

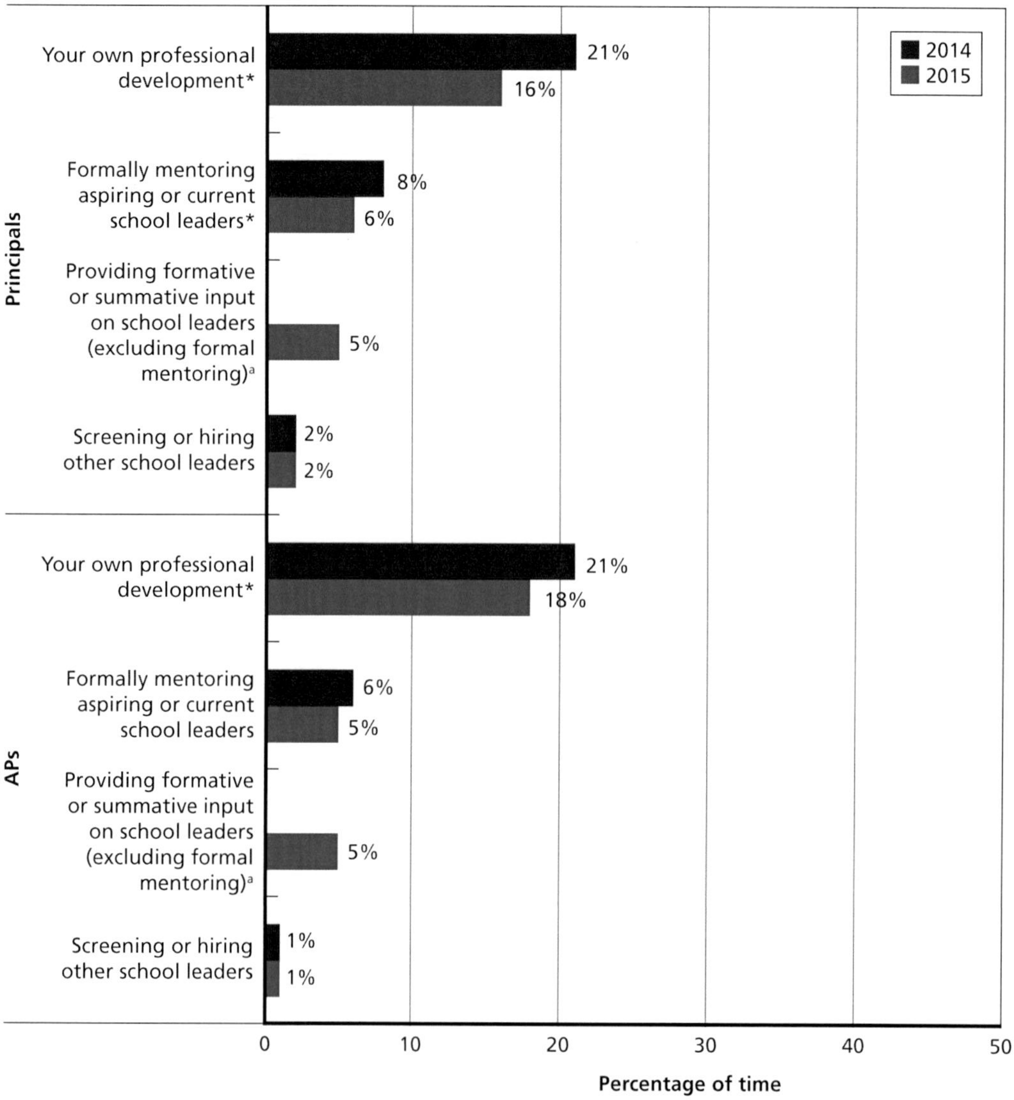

NOTE: * = significant difference between principal or AP reports in 2014 and 2015. The same school leaders did not necessarily complete the survey in both years. As discussed in Turnbull, Anderson, et al., 2016, Principal Pipeline Initiative districts used the terms *coaching* and *mentoring* to refer to individualized support or guidance provided to aspiring or current leaders. In this report, we do not distinguish between *mentoring* and *coaching* and use the phrase *mentoring and coaching* to refer to this broad category of support.

[a] No data was gathered in 2014 for this category.

Table 4.3
Average Percentage of Novice Principals in Principal Pipeline Initiative Districts Who Agreed with Survey Statements

Statement	Percentage Agreeing
The time I spend on activities to support the principal pipeline prevents me from attending to other important priorities at my school.	7.5
The time I spend on activities to support the principal pipeline enhances my ability to attend to important priorities at my school.	27.0

CHAPTER FIVE

Conclusions

This study employed an activity-based approach to understand the resources and expenditures used to improve and sustain a strong pipeline for preparing, hiring, supporting, and evaluating principals. For districts interested in undertaking similar efforts, our analysis provides a sense of what it takes to do this work to promote strong leadership in schools. In this chapter, we highlight some generalizable lessons that other districts might glean from the example of the districts participating in the Principal Pipeline Initiative.

Pipeline Spending Accounted for a Very Small Share of Participating Districts' Budgets

Our study shows that principal pipelines are not a big-ticket item for the participating school districts. On average, over the course of the initiative, participating districts devoted well under 1 percent (0.4 percent) of their expenditures to principal pipeline efforts, during a time when they were making active investments to enhance those pipelines. For all categories of principal pipeline activities and across all years of the initiative, districts spent about $5.6 million each year, on average. Their expenditures amounted to $42.30 per pupil or $31,243 per principal. To put these numbers into context, in the 2013–2014 SY, U.S. school districts (Cornman and Zhou, 2016, p. 13) spent, on average, $608 per pupil on school administration, $477 per pupil on transportation, and $447 per pupil on food services. Districts reported spending $23 per pupil supporting activities that are operated as businesses and generate revenue, such as after-school services.

Compared with other educational improvement initiatives for which resource requirements have been estimated, Principal Pipeline Initiative per-pupil pipeline expenditures are low. However, it should be noted that these other initiatives involve the delivery of education more directly and, for this reason, include the incremental cost of time for teachers and other school staff. Brewer et al., 1999, estimates the resources of class size reduction programs at $189 to $981 per pupil in 1998–1999 dollars, which would translate to $275 to $1,425 per pupil in 2015 dollars. Murphy and

Regenstein, 2012, estimates the costs of implementing the Common Core State Standards—including textbooks, assessments, and PD—at between about $250 and $400 per pupil, depending on the state.

Quick Pipeline Wins Will Not Break the Bank

Participating districts devoted the vast majority of pipeline resources to preservice preparation and on-the-job support and evaluation activities. These two major categories of pipeline activity accounted for three-quarters of all principal pipeline expenditures (almost $24,000 per principal). Perhaps more interesting for districts considering their own pipeline efforts is the finding that participating districts devoted modest resources to the development and revision of leader standards and to selective hiring and placement efforts—$0.41 per pupil ($292 per principal) and $3.57 per pupil ($2,894 per principal), respectively. These are activities that Turnbull, Anderson, et al., 2016, describes as quick wins, having high impact in participating districts.

Our findings thus suggest that a district does not need an infusion of substantial grant funding to make real progress on important aspects of principal pipelines. That said, leader standard development and selective hiring and placement are also areas in which the cost of district personnel time represents a large portion of expenditures. So although funding might not be a constraint in getting initiatives in areas of leader standards and hiring off the ground, district staff time could be. Indeed, in describing leader standards efforts, Turnbull, Anderson, et al., 2016, reports that "[d]eveloping and using standards required attention and effort over time, but district staff reported that the work had been worthwhile" (p. 13) and that "changes made in selection procedures and data systems took nontrivial amounts of staff time, both initially and on a continuing basis" (p. 33).

There Is Still Much to Learn About the Costs of Preservice Preparation and On-the-Job Support

Our analysis reveals substantial variation across districts in terms of spending on preservice preparation and on-the-job support. In general, participating districts devoted between 70 and 85 percent of pipeline resources to these two categories of activities combined. Readers might wonder whether any lessons in that variation point to cost-effective practices for preservice preparation and on-the-job support. Unfortunately, our study cannot provide definitive answers to that question. However, we do observe several issues that influence cost variation.

Depending on how districts configure their pipelines, on-the-job support for APs in one district might do the same work to improve leadership skills as preservice preparation activities intended to prepare APs for the principalship in another. This is evident from the fact that the share of pipeline resources devoted to preservice preparation ranged from a low of 11 percent in one district (where the share devoted to on-the-job support was 73 percent) to a high of 56 percent in one district (where the share devoted to on-the-job support was 27 percent). In the district with low preservice preparation expenditures, the district essentially provided principal preservice preparation through job-embedded training delivered to aspiring principals while they were working as APs.

Another issue influencing the level of reported expenditures in one district relative to that in another is whether the districts defined certain expenditures as part of the pipeline (or not). For example, one district undertook a reform of teacher positions during the initiative, creating teacher leader positions that would feed into the assistant principalship. That district felt very strongly that part of the expenditures associated with those positions was AP preservice preparation.

A third consideration influencing district-level expenditures on some major activities is the local context. Participating districts varied in terms of the depth of their pools of principal candidates at the launch of the initiative. Some of the districts had already been making investments to enhance the quality and size of their pools. Those districts invested in preservice preparation to keep the pool topped off. Other districts were making investments to fill the pool, and preservice preparation spending in those districts was greater.

Although our analysis did not allow us to identify best practices that could easily be transferred from one district to another, it does highlight some areas in which expenditures were relatively high and in which further examination of cost-effectiveness would be warranted. One such area is preservice preparation delivery. We found extremely wide variation across districts and within districts over time in expenditures devoted to preservice preparation, whether considered on a per-pupil, per-principal, or per-completer basis. Part of this difference might be due to differences in need, as described above. But we also found that that costs associated with residencies were a chief contributor to the total cost of preservice preparation. In one district, the cost of preservice preparation increased substantially when it increased the length of the residency in an ongoing program. That district viewed a longer residency as a quality enhancement and was eager to assess whether the additional cost of a longer residency was worth it.

With regard to both preservice preparation and on-the-job support and evaluation, participating districts engaged in a substantial amount of experimentation, as reflected by the share of expenditures devoted to activities that were characterized as investments in pipeline enhancements rather than ongoing. Over the course of the initiative, expenditures increased in both preservice preparation and on-the-job support and evaluation. But although expenditures directed to on-the-job support and evaluation remained stable over time, those devoted to preservice preparation declined at the end of the initiative. It is unclear why participating districts have pulled back on preservice preparation expenditures. It could be that a few of the districts had made investments to increase the size of the pool and, having done that, were limiting expenditures in this area. It could also be that districts had experimented with some preservice preparation activities and found that they did not work as well as they had hoped. Or some districts might have identified more cost-efficient ways to provide preservice preparation activities.

All Principal Pipeline Initiative Districts Made Investments in Systems and Capacity

Participating districts devoted at least some resources toward systems and capacity to support principal pipelines, including the development and maintenance of LTSs. Districts reported LTSs to be very useful, but their development required investments that varied a fair amount by district and by year, depending on the data resources that had already been developed in the district. On average, during the initiative, districts spent $1,990 per principal per year on LTSs, but those expenditures reached as much as $10,283 per principal, or a little over $2 million, in one year in one district. In total, districts spent on the order of $1 million to $2.5 million on LTSs over the course of the initiative. Also worth noting is that LTS development required personnel resources that were in limited supply or even unavailable in school districts. Thus, some of the resources necessary to develop and maintain the LTS were procured from outside consultants. LTS efforts thus likely involved at least some opportunity costs for the districts. Although participating districts benefited from technical assistance support, each district recognized the importance of ensuring that there was capacity within the district to take over the work eventually.

District Central Office Personnel Time Was a Key Pipeline Expenditure

Nearly half of the pipeline expenditures captured through our study were costs for the time of district personnel who led, guided, or contributed to principal pipeline activities. The cost of personnel time spent on pipeline activities amounted to almost $13,045 per principal per year, on average. In some ways, districts might perceive these expenditures for personnel time as easier to bear than other direct costs, such as the costs for consultants or subcontracts, as well as expenditures for materials and supplies. The personnel contributing to principal pipeline activities in each district were often district central office personnel who had been working in the district prior to the initiative or in positions that were present in the district prior to the initiative. Thus, districts might regard personnel expenditures as ones they would be paying regardless.

On the other hand, personnel costs represent a substantial time commitment on the part of district central office staff who have been identified as those who should focus on principal pipeline activities. Some of these staff took principal pipeline work on top of other duties and work that could be considered a full-time job already. Thus, as we have discussed, district personnel time devoted to the pipeline could represent an opportunity cost, in that it took time away from other activities that could have benefited the district.

Given increasing evidence that principal leadership matters a great deal for school outcomes, districts might want to consider how to reconfigure their offices—and, as a result, reconfigure district personnel time—to provide better preparation, hiring, and support for principals, as many participating districts have done. Thus, districts that wish to invest further in their principal pipelines might need to be particularly strategic in how they assign district staff to work on principal pipeline activities. For example, districts might consider how to assist those taking on key pipeline roles through provision of additional support staff, as well as whether they should develop new positions for those taking on key roles in pipeline work (e.g., directors of leadership development).

We also found that principals and APs spent at least some time doing things that contributed to the principal pipelines—they served as mentors for aspiring leaders, participated in the hiring process, and spent time on their own leadership development. Overall, principals reported that time spent on these activities enhanced rather than detracted from their work. However, it is important for districts to consider the trade-offs associated with asking principals to take time away from addressing the needs of their schools to support pipeline activities. In the survey, novice principals reported working 60 hours per week, on average. Taking on more pipeline responsibilities could crowd out other important school activities.

Cost Tools Created for This Study Might Be Useful to Other Districts

To inform this study, we developed data-collection tools that might be useful to other districts as they seek to identify the resources involved in building and maintaining comprehensive principal pipelines. The appendix includes a brief description of those tools and how they were used for our data collection. In applying such a tool in their own contexts, other districts would need to consider their own pipeline starting points and how they compare with those of participating districts.

The Experience of Principal Pipeline Initiative Districts Holds Lessons for Other Districts

This study provided expenditures for individual pipeline activities so that districts can consider the potential costs of those activities and whether to implement some pipeline activities and not others in their districts. However, districts should also be aware that many pipeline activities reinforce one another. Thus, the average expenditures for specific activities for participating districts could be influenced by district participation in other pipeline activities. For example, the time that districts invested in leader standards activities could have led to considerable decreases in the time that districts spent on other activities, such as the revision of preservice preparation or hiring and selection processes. Thus, districts that are considering improvements to their own principal pipelines should probably begin by considering overall strategies for pipeline improvements and their theories of action for connections among specific activities and expected outcomes. By doing such work, districts could potentially make more cost-efficient and cost-effective choices to improve and strengthen their principal pipelines.

The effect of the initiative investment is still unknown. For Turnbull, Anderson, et al., 2016, the authors found some suggestive evidence that initiative investments were leading to higher-quality new principals. They found that "more new principals over time said they were an 'excellent' fit for their schools, and district leaders saw greater strengths in their instructional leadership" (p. 55). They attribute the initiative's success in part to early investments in leader standards and hiring. The HR management literature suggests that investments in leader standards, selective hiring and placement, early-career mentoring and support, communication of clear expectations, evaluation against those expectations, and high-quality supervision have the potential to reduce principal turnover. A reduction in principal turnover could mean big savings for school districts. A report examining the initiative's effects will be released in 2018, providing more information for districts weighing investments in this area. It is too early to conclusively assess the implications that the initiative investments have for turnover in participating districts. However, our preliminary analysis of available data from participating districts suggests that, in three of the districts, the percentage of newly hired principals who continued to serve as principals in the district after two years increased substantially between 2010–2011 and 2013–2014.

APPENDIX

Technical Details on Data Collection and Analysis

This appendix includes more details about our data sources, data-collection tools, and analysis.

Data-Collection Tools

Our data-gathering began with the development of a Microsoft Excel template for tracking expenditures and associating them with major categories of pipeline activities and the activities and subactivities described in Table 2.1 in Chapter Two for each district. This data-collection tool is available for download as a spreadsheet from our website. This appendix provides a description of that tool. Table A.1 provides a snapshot of that template using fictional district data, focused on only one subactivity that falls under the larger activity of providing on-the-job support and induction for principals: providing principals with first-year induction and support. (The provision of on-the-job support for principals is an activity that is part of the on-the-job support and evaluation category.) The entire template includes highlighted rows listing each major category, activity, and subactivity included in the entire activity list in Table 2.1. We recorded any identified district expenditures under the appropriate subactivity and labeled them by academic year, by whether they were investment or ongoing expenditures, and by their cost type (including personnel, nonpersonnel, and various other cost types).

Although investment and ongoing expenditures for nonpersonnel costs were generally determined by the districts, we did query districts when their determinations were unclear to us. Based on feedback from points of contact in participating districts, we coded 50 percent of the cost of personnel on particular activities as an investment cost and 50 percent as an ongoing cost when those activities were focused more on revision or development of new systems. We did not code 100 percent of personnel costs for such activities as investment because we understood—from discussions with district personnel—that some portion of revision and development activities should be

Table A.1
Main Expenditure Data-Collection Tool Example

		SY 2011–2012 Expenditures, in Dollars	
	Cost Type	**Investment**	**Ongoing**
Component 4: On-the-job evaluation and support			
Activity: Provide on-the-job support and induction			
Subactivity: Provide principals with first-year induction and support			
Sent 20 principals to another school district to observe use of formative feedback	ODC: Travel	16,700	
Training stipends for ten principals serving as mentors for principal induction	Personnel: Internal staff salaries or stipends		30,000
District's state university provided facilities for first-year principal PD event	ODC: Facilities		1,000

expected to occur on an ongoing basis. The activities for which we categorized 50 percent of personnel time as investment and 50 percent as ongoing included the following:

- Develop or revise leader standards.
- Revise the system of preservice recruitment, selection, and preparation.
- Revise the system for principal recruiting, hiring, and placement.
- Revise the system for providing on-the-job support for principals and APs.
- Revise the system for providing evaluation to principals and APs.
- Revise the overall principal pipeline.
- Development and maintain an LTS.

We used a separate tool to gather information about district central office personnel time, and we then integrated that information into our main expenditure data–collection tool. To accurately track district personnel time investment in all principal pipeline activities—and the cost of that time—we created a template worksheet listing district personnel (or categories of personnel—e.g., those who supervise principals) who contributed any time to principal pipeline activities and their annual salary plus fringe benefits or the fringe benefit rate (so that we could calculate fringe benefits and add them to personnel salaries, the percentage of their district work hours spent on all principal pipeline activities combined, and the percentage of their work hours on principal pipeline activities spent on individual pipeline activities).

Table A.2 includes a snapshot of the template we used to capture district personnel time devoted to principal pipeline work, using fictional names and fictional data for one district and focusing on one category: selective hiring and placement. The whole personnel time expenditures template includes all principal pipeline cost activities. So, from this example, we can see that Jill Martin—a hypothetical district employee—spends 10 percent of time on activities devoted to the principal pipeline and that 10 percent can be divided among (1) designing new recruiting, hiring, and placement processes for school leaders (75 percent), (2) preparing and training personnel to use new processes and technology (20 percent), and (3) recruiting principal and AP candidates (5 percent). To calculate the cost of district personnel time on any

Table A.2
Principal Pipeline Personnel Time Expenditure Example

Name	Janice Brown	Jill Martin	
Position	Director of leadership initiatives	Director of HR	Associate deputy superintendents
Number of people	1	1	10
Percentage of all time spent on principal pipeline activities in SY 2011–2012	100	10	50
Annual salary for SY 2011–2012 (annual average salary for groups of personnel), in dollars	125,000	150,000	200,000
Activities to which personnel devoted time for SY 2011–2012 within component 3: selective hiring and placement, as percentages of time			
Design new recruiting, hiring, and placement processes, including technology and screening tools, for school leaders	10	75	
Prepare and train personnel to use new processes and technology for recruiting, hiring, and placing school leaders	5	20	
Recruit principal and AP candidates		5	
Screen and select candidates for candidate pool: Principals	5		
Screen and select candidates for candidate pool: APs	5		
Support and training for those in candidate pool	5		
Interview and hire school leaders: Principals			5
Interview and hire school leaders: APs			2

Table A.2—Continued

Name	Janice Brown	Jill Martin	
Position	Director of leadership initiatives	Director of HR	Associate deputy superintendents
Calculated cost of each activity for SY 2011–2012, in dollars			
Design new recruiting, hiring, and placement processes, including technology and screening tools, for school leaders	12,500	11,250	
Prepare and train personnel to use new processes and technology for recruiting, hiring, and placing school leaders	6,250	3,000	
Recruit principal and AP candidates		750	
Screen and select candidates for candidate pool: Principals	6,250		
Screen and select candidates for candidate pool: APs	6,250		
Support and training for those in candidate pool	6,250		
Interview and hire school leaders: Principals			50,000
Interview and hire school leaders: APs			20,000

activity, we multiplied the total percentage of the person's time on all pipeline activities by that person's salary and by the person's percentage of time spent on that particular activity. For example, to calculate the cost of Jill Martin's time recruiting principal and AP candidates, we used the following formula: 10% × $150,000 × 5% = $750. For cases in which groups of personnel were contributing time to the principal pipeline (e.g., associate deputy superintendents in Table A.2), we also multiplied the average salary for that group by the total number of people in that group and replaced the average salary estimate with the cumulative salary estimate in our formula.

We procured most of these percentage time estimates through interviews or structured interaction with our district points of contact, as well as interviews with district personnel. If someone found it too difficult to provide an exact estimate for the percentage of time spent on particular pipeline activities, we divided that percentage of effort equally among the activities in which that person was involved. We then incorporated personnel costs for each activity into our main expenditure data–collection tool.

In some cases, districts reported that personnel spent the same amount of time on particular revision activities (e.g., development of standards, revision of preservice preparation, revision of hiring systems) in each year. But when we queried some districts further, they reported that personnel spent much more time on some of these activities in some years. We therefore asked all district points of contact which years (between 2011–2012 and 2015–2016) were those years when certain activities were a particular focus for personnel. We then asked district points of contact to quantify the effort on those activities in some years compared with others.

References

Allen, David G., Phillip C. Bryant, and James M. Vardaman, "Retaining Talent: Replacing Misconceptions with Evidence-Based Strategies," *Academy of Management Perspectives*, Vol. 24, No. 2, May 2010, pp. 48–64.

Boushey, Heather, and Sarah Jane Glynn, "There Are Significant Business Costs to Replacing Employees," Center for American Progress, November 16, 2012. As of January 23, 2017:
https://www.americanprogress.org/issues/economy/reports/2012/11/16/44464/there-are-significant-business-costs-to-replacing-employees/

Brewer, Dominic J., Cathy Krop, Brian P. Gill, and Robert Reichardt, "Estimating the Cost of National Class Size Reductions Under Different Policy Alternatives," *Educational Evaluation and Policy Analysis*, Vol. 21, No. 2, Summer 1999, pp. 179–192.

Bureau of Economic Analysis, "GDP and Personal Income: Regional Data," undated. As of May 24, 2017:
https://www.bea.gov/iTable/iTable.cfm?reqid=70&step=1&isuri=1&acrdn=6#reqid=70&step=1&isuri=1

Burkhauser, Susan, "How Much Do School Principals Matter When It Comes to Teacher Working Conditions?" *Education Evaluation and Policy Analysis*, Vol. 39, No. 1, 2017, pp. 126–145.

Cascio, Wayne F., "The Economic Impact of Employee Behaviors on Organizational Performance," *California Management Review*, Vol. 48, No. 4, Summer 2006, pp. 41–59.

Chambers, Jay G., Irene Lam, and Kanya Mahitivanichcha, *Examining Context and Challenges in Measuring Investment in Professional Development: A Case Study of Six School Districts in the Southwest Region*, Regional Educational Laboratory Southwest, Issues and Answers REL 2008-No. 037, September 2008. As of May 23, 2017:
https://ies.ed.gov/ncee/edlabs/regions/southwest/pdf/REL_2008037.pdf

Cornman, Stephen Q., and Lei Zhou, *Revenues and Expenditures for Public Elementary and Secondary Education: School Year 2013–14 (Fiscal Year 2014)—First Look*, Washington, D.C.: U.S. Department of Education, National Center for Education Statistics, NCES 2016-301, October 2016. As of June 3, 2017:
https://nces.ed.gov/pubsearch/pubsinfo.asp?pubid=2016301

Darling-Hammond, Linda, Michelle LaPointe, Debra Meyerson, Margaret Terry Orr, and Carol Cohen, *Preparing School Leaders for a Changing World: Lessons from Exemplary Leadership Development Programs—Final Report*, Stanford, Calif.: Stanford University, Stanford Educational Leadership Institute, 2007. As of June 3, 2017:
http://www.wallacefoundation.org/knowledge-center/Documents/Preparing-School-Leaders.pdf

Discovery Education, "Evaluate Principal Effectiveness," undated.

Gates, Susan M., Laura S. Hamilton, Paco Martorell, Susan Burkhauser, Paul Heaton, Ashley Pierson, Matthew Baird, Mirka Vuollo, Jennifer J. Li, Diana Lavery, Melody Harvey, and Kun Gu, *Preparing Principals to Raise Student Achievement: Implementation and Effects of the New Leaders Program in Ten Districts*, Santa Monica, Calif.: RAND Corporation, RR-507-NL, 2014. As of October 25, 2016:
http://www.rand.org/pubs/research_reports/RR507.html

Gates, Susan M., Jeanne Ringel, Lucrecia Santibanez, Catherine H. Chung, and Karen E. Ross, *Who Is Leading Our Schools? An Overview of School Administrators and Their Careers*, Santa Monica, Calif.: RAND Corporation, MR-1679-EDU, 2003. As of October 25, 2016:
http://www.rand.org/pubs/monograph_reports/MR1679.html

George W. Bush Institute, *A Framework for Principal Talent Management*, Dallas, Texas, October 2016. As of January 23, 2017:
http://gwbcenter.imgix.net/Resources/gwbi-framework-principal-talent-mgmt.pdf

Gill, Jennifer, *Make Room for the Principal Supervisors*, New York: The Wallace Foundation, December 2013. As of May 23, 2017:
http://www.wallacefoundation.org/knowledge-center/Pages/Make-Room-for-the-Principal-Supervisors.aspx

———, *Chock Full of Data: How School Districts Are Building Leader Tracking Systems to Support Principal Pipelines*, New York: The Wallace Foundation, July 2016. As of May 23, 2017:
http://www.wallacefoundation.org/knowledge-center/Pages/Chock-Full-of-Data-How-School-Districts-Are-Building-Leader-Tracking-Systems-to-Support-Principal-Pipelines.aspx

Grissom, Jason A., "Can Good Principals Keep Teachers in Disadvantaged Schools? Linking Principal Effectiveness to Teacher Satisfaction and Turnover in Hard-to-Staff Environments," *Teachers College Record*, Vol. 113, No. 11, 2011, pp. 2552–2585.

Haberman, Michael, "Principal CEO," *Huffpost*, February 15, 2011. As of May 5, 2017:
http://www.huffingtonpost.com/Michael-Haberman/principal-ceo_b_823375.html

Haslam, M. Bruce, and Brenda J. Turnbull, "Research Brief: Costs of Participation in the School Administration Manager (SAM) Process," New York: The Wallace Foundation, August 2011. As of December 27, 2016:
http://www.wallacefoundation.org/knowledge-center/Documents/Research-Brief-Costs-of-Participation-in-the-School-Administration-Manager-(SAM)-Process.pdf

Herman, Rebecca, Susan M. Gates, Aziza Arifkhanova, Andriy Bega, Emilio Chavez-Herrerias, Eugene Han, Mark Harris, Jennifer Leschitz, and Stephani Wrabel, *School Leadership Interventions Under the Every Student Succeeds Act: Evidence Review—Updated and Expanded*, Santa Monica, Calif.: RAND Corporation, RR-1550-2-WF, 2017. As of May 23, 2017:
http://www.rand.org/pubs/research_reports/RR1550-2.html

Huselid, Mark A., Brian E. Becker, and Richard W. Beatty, *The Workforce Scorecard: Managing Human Capital to Execute Strategy*, Boston, Mass.: Harvard Business School Press, March 14, 2005.

Johnson, Gretchen, "From CSDs to CFNs: As the System for Providing Support Services to Schools Changed, Funding Levels Changed Too," New York: New York City Independent Budget Office, August 2014. As of December 22, 2016:
http://www.ibo.nyc.ny.us/iboreports/2014schoolsupportbudget.pdf

Johnson, Susan Moore, and Sarah E. Birkland, "The Schools That Teachers Choose," *Educational Leadership*, Vol. 60, No. 8, May 2003, pp. 20–24. As of June 3, 2017:
http://www.ascd.org/publications/educational-leadership/may03/vol60/num08/The-Schools-That-Teachers-Choose.aspx

Kaplan, Robert S., and Robin Cooper, *Cost and Effect: Using Integrated Cost Systems to Drive Profitability and Performance*, Boston, Mass.: Harvard Business School Press, 1998.

Lazear, Edward P., Kathryn L. Shaw, and Christopher T. Stanton, "The Value of Bosses," *Journal of Labor Economics*, Vol. 33, No. 4, October 2015, pp. 823–861.

Leithwood, Kenneth, Karen Seashore Louis, Stephen Anderson, and Kyla Wahlstrom, *How Leadership Influences Student Learning*, New York: Center for Applied Research and Educational Improvement, September 2004. As of May 23, 2017:
http://www.wallacefoundation.org/knowledge-center/Pages/How-Leadership-Influences-Student-Learning.aspx

Levenson, Nathan, Karla Baehr, James C. Smith, and Claire Sullivan, *Spending Money Wisely: Getting the Most from School District Budgets*, Boston, Mass.: District Management Council, 2014.

Levin, Henry M., and Patrick J. McEwan, *Cost-Effectiveness Analysis: Methods and Applications*, 2nd ed., Thousand Oaks, Calif.: Sage Publications, 2000.

Lincoln, Yvonna S., and Egon G. Guba, *Naturalistic Inquiry*, Thousand Oaks, Calif.: Sage Publications, 1985.

Manna, Paul, *Developing Excellent School Principals to Advance Teaching and Learning: Considerations for State Policy*, New York: The Wallace Foundation, September 2015. As of May 23, 2017:
http://www.wallacefoundation.org/knowledge-center/Pages/Developing-Excellent-School-Principals.aspx

Marzano, Robert J., Timothy Waters, and Brian A. McNulty, *School Leadership That Works: From Research to Results*, Alexandria, Va.: Association for Supervision and Curriculum Development, September 2005.

Mendels, Pamela, *Perspective: Building Principal Pipelines*, New York: The Wallace Foundation, October 2016. As of May 23, 2017:
http://www.wallacefoundation.org/knowledge-center/Pages/Perspective-Building-Principal-Pipelines.aspx

Miles, Karen Hawley, Allan Odden, Mark Fermanich, and Sarah Archibald, "Inside the Black Box of School District Spending on Professional Development: Lessons from Five Urban Districts," *Journal of Education Finance*, Vol. 30, No. 1, Summer 2004, pp. 1–26.

Mitgang, Lee, *Beyond the Pipeline: Getting the Principals We Need, Where They Are Needed Most*, New York: The Wallace Foundation, June 2003. As of May 23, 2017:
http://www.wallacefoundation.org/knowledge-center/Pages/Beyond-the-Pipeline-Getting-the-Principals-We-Need.aspx

Murphy, Patrick J., and Elliot Regenstein, *Putting a Price Tag on the Common Core: How Much Will Smart Implementation Cost?* Washington, D.C.: Thomas B. Fordham Institute, May 24, 2012. As of June 3, 2017:
https://edexcellence.net/publications/putting-a-price-tag-on-the-common-core.html

National Academies of Sciences, Engineering, and Medicine; Division of Behavioral and Social Sciences and Education; Board on Children, Youth, and Families; Committee on the Use of Economic Evidence to Inform Investments in Children, Youth, and Families, *Advancing the Power of Economic Evidence to Inform Investments in Children, Youth, and Families*, Washington, D.C.: National Academies Press, 2016. As of May 23, 2017:
https://www.nap.edu/catalog/23481/advancing-the-power-of-economic-evidence-to-inform-investments-in-children-youth-and-families

National Center for Education Statistics, "ElSi: Elementary/Secondary Information System," undated (a). As of May 24, 2017:
https://nces.ed.gov/ccd/elsi/

———, "Search for Public School Districts," undated (b). As of May 17, 2017:
https://nces.ed.gov/ccd/districtsearch/

———, "Enrollment, Poverty and Federal Funds for the 100 Largest School Districts, by Enrollment Size in 2012: Selected Years, 2011–12 Through 2014," *Digest of Education Statistics*, Table 215.30, Washington, D.C., May 2015. As of May 3, 2017:
https://nces.ed.gov/programs/digest/d14/tables/dt14_215.30.asp

National Policy Board for Educational Administration, *Professional Standards for Educational Leaders 2015*, Reston, Va., November 2015. As of May 23, 2017:
http://www.wallacefoundation.org/knowledge-center/Pages/Professional-Standards-for-Educational-Leaders-2015.aspx

National SAM Innovation Project, "What Is It Like to Be a SAM Principal?" Louisville, Ky., April 20, 2015. As of December 27, 2016:
http://www.samsconnect.com/?p=1134

NCES—*See* National Center for Education Statistics.

New Teacher Project, The, *The Mirage: Confronting the Hard Truth About Our Quest for Teacher Development*, August 4, 2015. As of May 23, 2017:
https://tntp.org/publications/view/the-mirage-confronting-the-truth-about-our-quest-for-teacher-development

O'Connor, John, "What Administrative Costs Say About School District Spending," *StateImpact*, May 2, 2012. As of December 27, 2016:
https://stateimpact.npr.org/florida/2012/05/02/what-administrative-costs-say-about-school-district-spending

Odden, Allan, Sarah Archibald, Mark Fermanich, and H. Alix Gallagher, "A Cost Framework for Professional Development," *Journal of Education Finance*, Vol. 28, No. 1, Summer 2002, pp. 51–74.

"Opportunity Cost," Investopedia, undated. As of May 23, 2017:
http://www.investopedia.com/terms/o/opportunitycost.asp

Porter, Andrew C., Joseph Murphy, Ellen Goldring, Stephen N. Elliott, Morgan S. Polikoff, and Henry May, *Vanderbilt Assessment of Leadership in Education: Technical Manual 1.0*, Nashville, Tenn.: Learning Sciences Institute, Vanderbilt University, November 2008. As of May 23, 2017:
http://www.wallacefoundation.org/knowledge-center/Pages/Vanderbilt-Assessment-of-Leadership-in-Education-Technical-Manual-1.aspx

Public Law 89-10, Elementary and Secondary Education Act, April 11, 1965.

Public Law 114-95, Every Student Succeeds Act, December 10, 2015. As of May 23, 2017:
https://www.gpo.gov/fdsys/search/pagedetails.action?collectionCode=PLAW&browsePath=114%2FPUBLIC%2F%5B0+-+99%5D&granuleId=&packageId=PLAW-114publ95&fromBrowse=true

Schaeffer, Adam B., "They Spend *What*? The Real Cost of Public Schools," *Policy Analysis*, No. 662, March 10, 2010. As of December 27, 2016:
https://www.cato.org/publications/policy-analysis/they-spend-what-real-cost-public-schools

School Leaders Network, *Churn: The High Cost of Principal Turnover*, 2014. As of December 27, 2016:
https://connectleadsucceed.org/churn_the_high_cost_of_principal_turnover

Smith, Morgan, "Do Texas Schools Spend Too Much on Administration?" *Texas Tribune*, February 25, 2011. As of December 22, 2016:
https://www.texastribune.org/2011/02/25/do-texas-schools-spend-too-much-on-administration/

Southern Regional Education Board, *The Three Essentials: Improving Schools Requires District Vision, District and State Support, and Principal Leadership*, Atlanta, Ga., August 2010. As of May 23, 2017:
http://www.wallacefoundation.org/knowledge-center/Documents/Three-Essentials-to-Improving-Schools.pdf

Strauss, Anselm L., and Juliet M. Corbin, *Basics of Qualitative Research: Techniques and Procedures for Developing Grounded Theory*, 2nd ed., Thousand Oaks, Calif.: Sage Publications, 1998.

Turnbull, Brenda J., Leslie A. Anderson, Derek L. Riley, Jaclyn R. MacFarlane, and Daniel K. Aladjem, *Building a Stronger Principalship*, Vol. 5: *The Principal Pipeline Initiative in Action*, Washington, D.C.: Policy Studies Associates, October 2016. As of May 23, 2017:
http://www.wallacefoundation.org/knowledge-center/Pages/Building-a-Stronger-Principalship-Vol-5-The-Principal-Pipeline-Initiative-in-Action.aspx

Turnbull, Brenda J., M. Bruce Haslam, Erikson R. Arcaira, Derek L. Riley, Beth Sinclair, and Stephen Coleman, *Evaluation of the School Administration Manager Project*, Washington, D.C.: The Wallace Foundation, December 2009. As of December 27, 2016:
http://www.wallacefoundation.org/knowledge-center/Documents/Evaluation-of-the-School-Administration-Manager-Project.pdf

Turnbull, Brenda J., Derek L. Riley, Erikson R. Arcaira, Leslie M. Anderson, and Jaclyn R. MacFarlane, *Six Districts Begin the Principal Pipeline Initiative*, Washington, D.C.: Policy Studies Associates, July 2013. As of May 23, 2017:
http://www.wallacefoundation.org/knowledge-center/Pages/Six-Districts-Begin-the-Principal-Pipeline-Initiative.aspx

Turnbull, Brenda J., Derek L. Riley, and Jaclyn R. MacFarlane, *Building a Stronger Principalship*, Vol. 2: *Cultivating Talent Through a Principal Pipeline*, Washington, D.C.: Policy Studies Associates, December 2013. As of November 11, 2016:
http://www.wallacefoundation.org/knowledge-center/Pages/Building-a-Stronger-Principalship-Vol-2-Cultivating-Talent-Through-a-Principal-Pipeline.aspx

———, *Building a Stronger Principalship*, Vol. 3: *Districts Taking Charge of the Principal Pipeline*, Washington D.C.: Policy Studies and Associates, January 2015. As of May 23, 2017:
http://www.wallacefoundation.org/knowledge-center/Pages/Building-a-Stronger-Principalship-Vol3-Districts-Taking-Charge.aspx

U.S. Department of Education, *Non-Regulatory Guidance: Using Evidence to Strengthen Education Investments*, Washington, D.C., September 16, 2016a. As of May 23, 2017:
https://www2.ed.gov/policy/elsec/leg/essa/guidanceuseseinvestment.pdf

———, *Non-Regulatory Guidance for Title II, Part A: Building Systems of Support for Excellent Teaching and Leading*, Washington, D.C., September 27, 2016b. As of May 23, 2017:
https://www2.ed.gov/policy/elsec/leg/essa/essatitleiipartaguidance.pdf

Wakefield, Nicky, Anthony Abbatiello, Dimple Agarwal, Karen Pastakia, and Ardie van Berkel, "Leadership Awakened: Generations, Teams, Science," in *Global Human Capital Trends 2016: The New Organization—Different by Design*, Deloitte University Press, February 26, 2016, pp. 27–36. As of May 23, 2017:
https://dupress.deloitte.com/dup-us-en/focus/human-capital-trends/2016/identifying-future-business-leaders-leadership.html

Wallace Foundation, The, "Knowledge Center: Building a Stronger Principalship," undated. As of May 23, 2017:
http://www.wallacefoundation.org/knowledge-center/Pages/Building-a-Stronger-Principalship.aspx

———, "The Wallace Foundation Launches Major 'Principal Pipeline' Initiative to Help School Districts Build a Corps of Effective School Principals," press release, August 22, 2011. As of May 24, 2017:
http://www.wallacefoundation.org/News-and-Media/press-releases/Pages/The-Wallace-Foundation-Launches-Major-Principal-Pipeline-Initiative-to-Help-School-Districts-Build-Corps.aspx

———, "Wallace Invests $30 Million to Strengthen Supervisors of School Principals to Improve Their Ability to Lead Schools," press release, June 24, 2014. As of May 24, 2017:
http://www.wallacefoundation.org/News-and-Media/press-releases/Pages/Wallace-Invests-$30-Million-to-Strengthen-Supervisors.aspx

———, "Building a Stronger Principalship," web page, 2015–2017. As of June 14, 2017:
http://www.wallacefoundation.org/knowledge-center/Pages/Building-a-Stronger-Principalship.aspx

Waters, Tim, Robert J. Marzano, and Brian McNulty, *Balanced Leadership™: What 30 Years of Research Tells Us About the Effect of Leadership on Student Achievement*, Denver, Colo.: McREL International, June 27, 2003. As of May 23, 2017:
https://www.mcrel.org/balanced-leadership-what-30-years-of-research-tells-us-about-the-effect-of-leadership-on-student-achievement-2003/

Watlington, Eliah, Robert Shockley, Paul Guglielmino, and Rivka Felsher, "The High Cost of Leaving: An Analysis of the Cost of Teacher Turnover," *Journal of Education Finance*, Vol. 36, No. 1, Summer 2010, pp. 22–37.

Williamson, Oliver E., "The Theory of the Firm as Governance Structure: From Choice to Contract," *Journal of Economic Perspectives*, Vol. 16, No. 3, Summer 2002, pp. 171–195.